The

Guide to the Toddler Years

Professional, reassuring advice on surviving–and thriving– during the toddler years!

Rebecca Rutledge, Ph.D.

SOURCEBOOKS, INC.®
NAPERVILLE, ILLINOIS

Published by Sourcebooks, Inc.
P.O. Box 4410, Naperville, Illinois 60567-4410
(630) 961-3900
Fax: (630) 961-2168
www.sourcebooks.com

Library of Congress Cataloging-in-Publication Data
Rutledge, Rebecca.
  Playskool guide to the toddler years : from together time to temper tantrums, practical advice to fully enjoy your toddler's wonder years / Rebecca Rutledge.
      p. cm.
  Includes index.
  ISBN 978-1-4022-0932-1 (trade pbk.)
  1. Toddlers–Development. 2. Child development. 3. Parenting. I. Title.
HQ774.5.R87 2007
305.231–dc22
                                        2007020083

Printed and bound in the United States of America.
BG 10 9 8 7 6 5 4 3 2

Contents

Introduction

Welcome to the wonderful world of toddlers! As a psychologist, I find this group of little people to be a fascinating age group, along with adolescents, who possess many of the same characteristics!

If you are lucky enough to be blessed with a child who is entering the toddler years, you are embarking on a wild, wonderful, and wacky adventure. I think all of the traits of a toddler are well-captured by the simple description below.

Terrific

Orangutan

Delightful

Devious

Loving

Enthusiastic

Rambunctious Rascal

Toddlers are **terrific**! Well, not all the time, but they are terribly entertaining and fun. When you have a toddler around, you are never at a loss for something to do, whether it is banging on a pot alongside her or watching her eat spaghetti. Everything she does will be new and great!

Your toddler may remind you of an **orangutan**. Toddlers will climb anything, and they can move their bodies in ways we grown-ups have long forgotten. Just like orangutans, they can bite their own toes! They will clap and scratch and pick at you, and they find their bodies endlessly mesmerizing!

A toddler is **delightful**. When your toddler smiles at you, your heart melts and you'll be absolutely convinced she is *the* most beautiful toddler in the whole wide world. Her ability to turn the most minor thing into a major discovery amazes you. Her giggle is infectious. Everything she does reminds you how wonderful it is to be alive.

A toddler can also be a tiny bit **devious**. Given the chance, she can find trouble in the strangest places. Everything is fair game for mischief. She doesn't always mean to get into trouble—she just does! Her job is to try new things, and that means touching, throwing, kicking, running, and hitting—well, you get the idea. If it exists, she *must* try it! Your job is to be patient and try not to pull all of your hair out.

A toddler is **loving**. When was the last time you got a hug from your toddler? When those arms reach around and grab you tightly, there's no other feeling like it. He can make you feel as if you are the most important person in his life!

A toddler is **enthusiastic**. Toddlers remind us of the joy we can find in just about anything if we look hard enough. Your toddler will be equally excited by his new toy and the container it came in. He will be pretty sure he is the first person who learned how to poop in a potty! That little mole on the back of your neck can provide at least a few minutes of quiet as he inspects it very carefully.

A toddler is also a **rambunctious rascal,** full of energy and fun. Her desire to learn new things and explore her world will overwhelm and astound you. She might wear you down and wear you out, but she will always find a way to make you smile.

So there you have it! Raising your toddler is both a privilege and a responsibility. His mere presence will make you feel that you are blessed beyond comparison. You will have the privilege of teaching him about life while he teaches you a thing or two as well. Your responsibility is to take care of him, nurture him, and love him so that he will grow to be a healthy, happy, and loving adult. Once you have a toddler, you will wonder how you ever got along without one. Enjoy!

Rebecca Rutledge

Developmental Timeline

The following is a basic timeline of what your toddler may be doing at a given age. Keep in mind, however, that knowing where a toddler should be developmentally is not an *exact* science. Your toddler may be ahead of the timeline, and another child may be slightly or even further behind it—which in most cases is just fine. Do not panic if your toddler doesn't appear to be growing at the "perfect" rate! Your toddler is a human being, after all, and her development has a schedule all its own. Unless there is a specific developmental problem, don't worry too much if your toddler can't perform a particular task yet; as with almost everything, your toddler will do it when *she* is good and ready!

13 Months
- Put herself into a sitting position
- Pull up to stand and stand alone
- Move from object to object while holding onto something for stability
- Clap hands
- Communicate in ways besides crying to tell you what she wants
- Drink from a cup
- Use one to two recognizable words

- Point
- Imitate some behaviors
- Put one object into another (e.g., block into a cup)
- Remove a small article of clothing
- Knows at least one body part

14 Months

- Stand and walk alone
- Possibly run
- Possibly walk up steps with help
- Bend over and pick things up
- Build with one to two blocks
- Wave bye-bye
- Use three to six words, use the words for Mom and Dad on purpose to get parents' attention
- Follow one- to two-step verbal requests

15 Months

- Use a spoon and a fork (although hands remain primary eating tools)
- Imitate behaviors with a doll
- Scribble
- Communicate emotions such as pleasure, interest, etc.

16 Months

- Kick a ball
- Brush teeth with help
- Scribble
- Use at least six words

17 Months

- Throw a ball overhead
- Build a tower with two to three objects
- Speak more clearly

• Combine two words
• Name or point as if to identify two objects in a picture book
• Remove an article of clothing
• Walk up steps

18 Months to 20 Months

• Communicate wants, use about 50 single words
• Imitate acts with dolls and toys
• Wash and dry hands
• Build a tower of two to four blocks
• Name about six body parts
• Zip clothing, such as jackets
• Identify objects by pointing
• Begin teething
• Show interest in potty training

20 Months to 24 Months

• Put on one simple piece of clothing (e.g., a sock)
• Jump up and down
• Combine two to four words
• Use prepositions (under, on, etc.)
• May be able to talk using two to three sentences
• Build a tower with six to eight objects
• Draw a line in imitation
• More interest in potty training

25 Months to 30 Months

• Name a friend
• Describe what an object can do
• Balance on one foot for one to two seconds
• Jump forward
• Name one color

30 Months to 33 Months

- Count one object
- Use one to two adjectives
- Carry on short conversations
- Balance on one foot for two to three seconds
- Put on a shirt

33 Months to 36 Months

- Put cereal in a bowl
- Dress without help (although clothing may not match!)
- Name four colors
- Draw a circle (sort of!)

36 Months to 40 Months

- Show increased signs of independence (although separation issues will likely still be common)
- Toileting accidents after toilet training is complete
- Talk to himself
- Eat mostly with utensils (although he will still play with food)
- Move from crib to bed

40 Months to 45 Months

- Begin establishing relationships with peers
- Refuse to obey
- Tantrums
- Development of fears and phobias
- Fantasy play (let's pretend)
- Imaginary friends
- Eat with utensils

45 Months to 48 Months

- Increase in independence
- Ability to argue with you
- Further development of fears and phobias
- Can repeat a story
- Make friends

Part One

The Wonderful Ones
(12–24 Months)

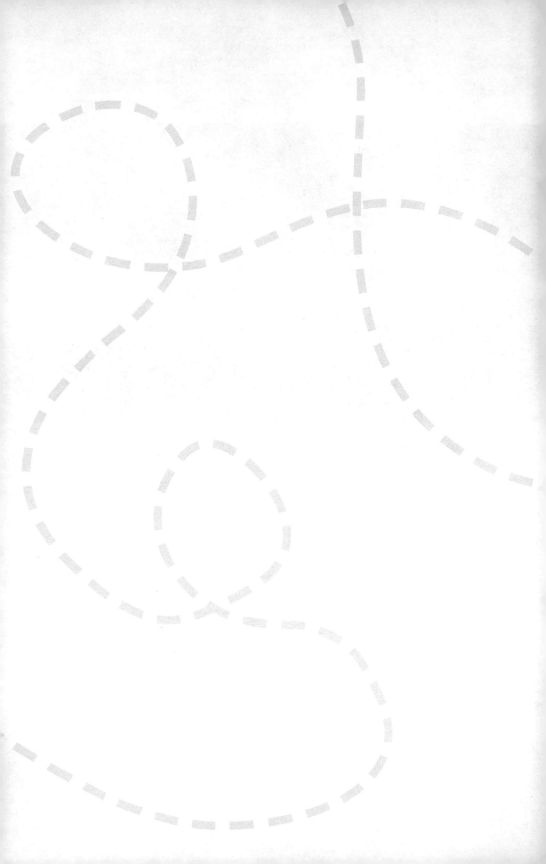

Growing and Going!

Here you go! You and your toddler are about to embark on an endless journey of trials, tribulations, and joys. Everything he does will be new to him, so it will feel new to you as well.

Getting Around

The first sign of independence for toddlers between the ages of 12 months and 24 months is walking. Once this is mastered, watch out!

Crawling before Walking

One of the most exciting milestones for you as a parent will be seeing your child take his first steps. The accomplishment can also be somewhat daunting, because trying to keep him corralled can be a challenge! Most kids learn how to crawl at around nine months, and walking begins to occur between 13 and 15 months. Walking independently doesn't happen all at once, however, because there are several skills your toddler must master first. In addition, your child might alternate between crawling and walking for some period of time before he is ready to become a full-fledged walker.

The first sign that your toddler is getting ready to begin walking is that he will hold firmly to a support object, such as a chair or a coffee table, and pull himself up to a standing position. The object will hold his weight, and if he moves, he will not take his hands off but will instead move sideways so as not to lose contact. Once he is a little more confident, he might pull back from his support object and try supporting all of his weight on his own, but those little hands will remain on the support to keep him balanced.

If there are some support objects that are relatively close together, such as the sofa and the coffee table, he will begin to navigate between the objects, with one hand always holding on for safety. You might want to create an environment of closely positioned support objects if one doesn't exist already so that he can master this new skill when he is ready.

The next part of learning to walk can be scary for you as a parent to watch, but it is a necessary skill for your child to learn. If your toddler spots something he wants, he will try to figure out how to get to it, but only if he continues to have support. When the space between support objects is too large, however, your toddler will be tempted to take a couple of steps on his own. You do not need to force this; your child will decide when he is ready to take that new risk. As long as he is somewhat protected from hurting himself, you need to let him do it on his own. If he falls, don't rush in to rescue him unless he is truly hurt. Remember, we *really do* have to learn to crawl before we can walk, and there is a method to this madness!

Walking

Once these skills have been learned, your toddler will be ready to start taking steps on his own. You've probably observed babies who are beginning to walk. They look like noodles, curling and bending and drooping all over the place. They are wobbly, unco-ordinated, and actually sort of goofy-looking. This is perfectly natural, as this is the time they are learning coordination and balance. Some children take longer to develop coordination than do others, but each child will usually set his own pace, and there is not much you can do to hurry this along or to slow it down.

During this time, your presence is crucial to your toddler's feelings of security. If you change locations or disappear from sight, it can be incredibly frustrating and scary for him! He does not want you to move at all. If you decide to move, you'll find that your toddler won't follow you but will raise his arms for you to carry him. This is normal developmentally, so don't be impatient or irritated. He won't learn to follow you until he's a bit older.

> As your toddler begins learning to walk, he will take steps away from you, but research shows that during this time, toddlers will rarely go where they cannot keep you in full view.

Climbing

Now that he's got that walking trick down, the next new and exciting activity your toddler will learn is climbing. He will be much more excited and curious about this than you will be, but he is going to do it whether you like it or not! At about the age of 15 months, a child will climb using his hands. In other words, he won't realize that he can use his hands *and* his feet at the same time to reach his destination. Climbing becomes more dangerous a few months later, when he finally figures out that he has to use his hands and feet together to reach what it is that he wants. The problem with the newly successful climber is that he will sit wherever he chooses and whenever he feels like it. It does not occur to him that he cannot climb up a set of steps and then sit backward without falling. So while you want to encourage climbing as a natural part of learning to get around, you'll need to remain close for safety.

Running

You'll notice at around 24 months that your toddler is running much as he used to walk. He will fall down and appear uncoordinated, and you may begin to worry that there is something wrong. It takes time, energy, and focus for these little people to learn the task of walking and climbing and running. Your toddler is not concerned about whether he's coordinated—he simply wants to get to another spot! He is learning by the act of doing, and unless he is in danger of being hurt, you're going to have to leave him alone.

Back to Crawling

Don't be alarmed if your toddler regresses at times and begins to crawl again. This can happen for any number of reasons. Your toddler may have taken a bit of a rough tumble and gotten scared. Other toddlers crawl when they are not confident about walking. For example, if your toddler is in a new situation, such as being in another relative's home or on vacation, he may feel unsure about his ability to walk and will begin to crawl again. There is no need, however, to worry that your child will continue to crawl until he is five years old! As you are no doubt learning, toddlers have minds of their own, and they will get up and walk again when they are good and ready.

Helping Your Toddler as He Learns

There are some fun activities that you can do with your toddler as he begins this new adventure. One is to play pull-up games with him. If he is showing signs that he is ready to stand, there's nothing wrong with holding out your hands and pulling him into a standing position. Praise him and communicate that this is fun and exciting. The key is to help him see that this is a positive experience and one that you are enjoying as well.

This is the perfect time to provide him with a toy lawn mower, grocery cart, or the like, which he can use for support. This will also help him learn to incorporate play into his new upright position!

Toddlers at this age rarely walk with toys in their hands because they are focused on just trying to learn to stand on their own. You'll notice that if your child wants to play with a toy, he will sit down and engage in play, but he will drop the toy or whatever he is doing so that he can begin walking again.

Getting Your Toddler to Sleep

By now you have had your share of sleepless nights followed by days spent draped in a complete fog. Amazingly enough, however, you *are* still standing—a good thing, because you have more sleepless nights to come! On average, toddlers need about 10 to 12 hours of sleep per day. Note this is per *24-hour day*, not all at night. It is necessary for you to impose some sort of sleep schedule if you want to be alert and able to keep up!

Setting a Sleep Routine for Your Toddler

The question most parents will ask is whether a strict routine is absolutely necessary for toddlers. While some experts believe that a sleep routine is crucial, others don't emphasize it as much. The real answer lies in your daily routine and schedule. Toddlers become quite cranky and unpleasant when they have not had their sleep. If your schedule is one in which there is a lot of unpredictability, this can affect your toddler and, ultimately, you. On the other hand, if you have a toddler who manages to sleep whenever he can, including catnapping when you are on the go, a strict routine may not be as important for your family. The bottom line is that having no routine at all won't cause long-term damage, but it will probably be very hard for you and your toddler in the short run.

Between the ages of 12 months and 18 months, most toddlers need about two naps a day to keep them going. What times the naps should occur will be up to your toddler. You'll need to observe

> Developing a sleep routine for your toddler is easier and less stressful than a haphazard approach, and it will give you some much-needed predictability.

when he eats, when he becomes sleepy, and when he is at his most active. Your toddler will more or less let you know when he wants to nap. This does not mean that he will tell you he is sleepy, but his behavior will begin to communicate it with some regularity, and then you can determine when naptime is most appropriate. Generally, your toddler will take one nap in the morning and another in the afternoon. As he gets closer to 24 months, one nap will become sufficient.

Wake Him or Let Him Sleep?

Parents often ask whether they should let a child sleep as long as he wishes or wake him after a set time period. There are few parents who don't love it when their child takes an exceptionally long nap, so that they can get a break! Allowing this to happen occasionally is fine. For the most part, you'll need to find out what works best for your child. Typically, if your child sleeps longer than an hour or so at each naptime, it may be harder to get him to bed at a reasonable hour. But if you find yourself having to wake him on a daily basis, he may simply be trying to let you know that he needs more sleep. What you have to remember is that just as with adults, your toddler's sleep needs may change depending on what is going on that day. When it comes to bedtime routines, most authorities agree that you will have an easier time establishing a sleep schedule for your child if you wake him at the same time each day and get him to bed at the same time each night. Unlike naptimes, a schedule is more important for waking and going to bed at night to ensure that he gets enough sleep, and that you get your rest as well.

Bedtime Fussiness

Do not believe for a minute that your toddler will be *the* one who never fusses about going to bed! All toddlers protest at one point or another about heading off to bed, particularly if they think they are missing something. If possible, keep evenings as calm and uneventful as you can. Start developing a routine to prepare your toddler for sleep. For some, this might be a warm bubble bath. However, if your toddler loves playing in the water and finds it to be incredibly exciting, a bath may not be the best way to end his day! As you are putting on his pajamas, you might dim the lights or put on some calming music that he enjoys.

Getting Your Toddler to Fall Asleep on His Own

Your toddler *does* need to learn to fall asleep on his own. Bedtime is often when most parents like to coddle their toddlers, rock them to sleep, and even curl up with them until they fall asleep. Believe it or not, this is not the best strategy. You may be saying, "But he falls asleep the minute I begin to rock him." You're probably right, and this is much like putting a child in the car and having the sound of the motor lull him off before you even get out of the driveway. But have you noticed that more often than not when you stop rocking and move him to his bed he jolts awake? You'll find yourself having to rock him again, and you may go through this activity several times before he is finally really asleep. This is not a

Teaching your toddler to fall asleep by himself requires as few interruptions from you as possible. If he is having trouble getting to sleep on his own, and you let him use a bottle to soothe himself, he's going to expect another bottle when he awakes. Once again, you'll have to intervene regularly, which causes less uninterrupted sleep for him and for you.

recommendation against rocking or other bonding moments with your toddler before he falls asleep. If you are going to do some of these activities at bedtime, make it a part of the sleep preparation time, not as the only way he knows how to go to sleep.

Is "Crying It Out" Okay?

Letting your toddler "cry it out" until he falls asleep is not the best for him psychologically. Toddlers have only recently begun to navigate in their new little worlds. While they are curious, they are also anxious and insecure about their new experiences. Leaving a toddler to cry on his own until he simply wears himself out sends him the message, "I'm gone. You're all alone. Good luck." Not only does this leave him feeling scared, angry, and anxious, but it also will encourage him to begin wandering from his bed. Remember, he needs you, and if he perceives you to be far away from him, he's going to go in search of you.

A better way to handle a toddler who cries at bedtime is to be firm, but cheerful. While you don't want to let yourself become a hostage to his crying, you do need to be available to soothe him if necessary. When he begins to whimper, simply tell him that you are close by, and that it is time for everyone to go to sleep. Once you put him into his bed, don't dawdle. Cheerfully call out good night and leave the room.

At bedtime, reassure your toddler cheerfully as you go along with your routine of preparing him for sleep.

When he begins to cry, you'll have to assess whether or not these are cries of protest because he does not want to be left alone or go to sleep. Try waiting for at least three minutes before going in to check on him. This will seem like an eternity to you at first, but you need to see if he will simply stop crying and soothe himself to sleep. If the crying has not stopped, it's time for you to reenter his room to repeat that everything is fine and it's time for sleep. Do not fall for his cuteness! He is going to try and be as adorable as possible to get you to want to interact with him. This is not time for fun, and he needs to get that message. You should stay in his room approximately 30 seconds to reassure him, and then leave again.

This routine will be difficult to establish at first, but once you have done so, you'll be glad your child has a sleep schedule. If the crying doesn't die down after a week or so, you might try sitting in a chair close to the bed; however, do not interact with your child. Be sure to remain quiet. It's important that you keep your distance so that he understands it is time for bed, not playtime.

Waking During the Night

When your child wakes up at night, it is typical for him to be scared. There are several things that you can do to minimize your involvement. For example, if he has a favorite blanket, make sure that it is available in his bed. If he is still using his pacifier, you might put an extra one in his bed where he can find it. A nightlight often helps when toddlers awaken to find themselves in the dark. If these alternatives don't work, then you will need to go in and soothe him for 30 seconds as you did while trying to get him to sleep.

A great activity to begin preparing your child for sleep is discussing bedtime at dinnertime. Talk about how much fun it is to curl up with a blanket and to go "night night." This is a great time to encourage your child to pick out a "baby" that he can sleep with—a stuffed animal, blanket, or doll, for example. As you are preparing for bed, make the "baby" a part of the routine.

Toddler Nightmares

Do toddlers have nightmares? Yes, they do, but the fear you may see on your child's face is more likely a result of awakening and not being comfortable in his surroundings. Toddlers who do have nightmares are usually overtired or are experiencing stress of some kind. For example, a toddler may be in a completely new environment, or the usual routines in the house may have been unsettled, such as by the arrival of a new baby.. Simply maintain your habit of briefly soothing your toddler and letting him get back to sleep as soon as possible.

The Importance of Consistency

Consistency really is the key to getting your toddler to fall asleep on his own and stay in his bed. Some children seem to fall effortlessly into the routine you have established and have little difficulties with it. For those parents who have succeeded with this easily—congratulations! For the rest of you—keep dreaming and keep trying! Usually toddlers are fairly resistant to the schedule being imposed on them. It'll be up to you to assess whether your child simply does not want to go to bed or the schedule needs to be altered.

Picky Eater or Normal Appetite?

You've observed other parents having this problem, and you might even be one of those parents yourself. You can't get your child to eat! This can be an extremely worrisome experience for many parents because, of course, they want their child to be well nourished and healthy. As you've no doubt learned, toddlers have their own unique ways of going about things, and eating can quickly become a major battle.

Grown-Up Food

Between the ages of 12 months and 24 months, your toddler is probably ready to begin eating what your family eats. You'll have to make a transition between baby food and grown-up food, and for a while your toddler might eat some of both. He will change to regular food more quickly if the food is easy to eat (as when cut into small pieces) and easy to handle. He will eat like a barbarian, using his fists and fingers, or even placing his mouth on his plate! Although this might drive you crazy, and you may be tempted to feed him yourself, don't do it. Part of what you are teaching your child is that eating is pleasurable, and he should eat when he is hungry, not as a result of your begging or cajoling him.

Eating Battles

Do not get drawn into eating battles with your child. Eating and being with the family should be an enjoyable activity, not one filled with struggles over whether your toddler is eating the right foods in the right manner. Your toddler is struggling for some independence and autonomy, and this is one activity that he certainly has control over! Therefore, begging him to eat or forcing him to try "just a bite" can very easily backfire. Let him stop when he feels full, and let him eat his food in any combination or order he wishes. That includes dessert. What? Dessert before peas? Toddlers don't understand the practice of eating certain foods before others. They don't care, and mostly they just want to eat if they are hungry. The time will come later for you to teach him about manners and that dessert doesn't come first. For now, understand that he *is* eating, and isn't that what you wanted in the first place?

> When it comes to your toddler's eating, you'll do well to learn this important lesson: kids really *do* eat when they're hungry! They're not going to let themselves starve, so back off, enjoy your mealtime with your toddler, and save the battles for other issues.

Snacking

Most parents worry that their children are snacking too much if they do not eat their dinner. For toddlers, this is *not* the case. Toddlers need the extra energy that comes along with snacks during the day. Your job is to try to make the snacks healthy as possible. This means limiting fast food, candy, and sodas, which have a short-term energizing effect but lack adequate nutritional benefits and end up making your child hungrier in the long run. Make sure your child's snacks are not nearly as yummy as what you are serving for dinner. This will keep your toddler from subsisting on snacks rather than on regular meals.

Managing Teething

On average, a toddler gets her first tooth between four months and seven months. Her first molars come in between 13 months and 19 months. These teeth are twice as hard to cut as her incisors, so the teething process is much more painful and uncomfortable.

> Teething can be the perfect time to teach your toddler about dental hygiene. Have him look in the mirror and try to count his teeth. Let him pick out his own toothpaste and toothbrush. Make brushing his teeth part of his bedtime ritual.

All you can do to help your child feel better is try to decrease the pain somehow. This can be done by using one of the teething gels that are on the market. Rubbing your finger along the gum may help, but most toddlers don't want you to go near their mouths at this time. A frozen teething ring is probably the best tool to use because it is solid and, when cold, it will numb the pain. Sugar-free popsicles are another tasty alternative.

If your pediatrician okays it, baby aspirin sometimes helps with the pain. And although your grandmother may have used this remedy on you, using alcohol is *not* recommended.

Is It Time for Toilet Training?

Although you can probably hardly wait for your toddler to be free of diapers, once again, she will be the one to let you know that she is ready for this next step. Generally, when a child is 18 to 20 months old, she simply cannot control her bladder. Her bowel movements may become regular before her urination schedule. When your toddler can stay dry for about two hours, she may be ready to start toilet training. Also, when having a wet, full, and dirty diaper becomes frustrating to her, that is another encouraging sign. If she begins to imitate you by pulling on her pants or copying what you are doing in the bathroom, she is beginning to show some curiosity. Another behavior you might notice is squatting while having a bowel movement.

If you feel that your toddler is showing signs of being ready to begin toilet training, start using words to communicate what she will be doing—"tee tee," "poop," etc. If you prefer, use the correct words, but children seem to respond better to the silly phraseology. Do not rush this process. Doing so will only result in failure because your toddler won't be ready for this big step. Trust that she will let you know when the time is right for her, and don't push her. This is another area in which she has complete control, and she needs to exert that authority. She won't be in diapers forever, but she also won't let you be the one to make the decision about when she's ready to use the potty on her own.

2

Cognitive Changes

Learning to Play

While your toddler is learning new physical activities such as walking, she is also learning to play. At this stage, a toddler does not understand cause and effect. She is only focused on is what is happening to her at that moment. If an activity is not interesting, she is not going to try it. Between the ages of 12 and 18 months, play becomes a game of exploration. If you have spent any time around toddlers, you've noticed that they like to touch, taste, squeeze, and drop just about any object within their grasp. Objects that older children would not find enjoyable are fascinating to toddlers. Have you ever bought a toy for your child, only to find that she likes the box better than the toy in it? Who wouldn't find putting a box on one's head or climbing into it fun and exciting?

During this time, your toddler is capable of learning simple games such as patty-cake or waving "bye-bye." She will begin experimenting with putting objects into other objects; for example, she will put water into a cup or sand into a bucket. She will repeatedly drop things or throw them down. She may not understand yet that these objects are not going to miraculously pop

Anything can be a toy to a toddler—a stick, a spoon, a box, a shoe. It's all new, and it's all educational. By paying attention to what your child is drawn to, you can provide her with other similar objects that might be entertaining.

back up into her hands. If she seems interested, give her a large crayon with which she can scribble—just make sure she tries this out on paper and not on your living-room walls!

At about 18 months, your toddler's understanding of cause and effect may start to develop. She may begin taking one block and placing it on top of another one. She may discover that when she knocks the top block off, it falls onto the floor. She may recall that this is similar to when she drops something from her high chair onto the floor. All of a sudden, she realizes that she has to actively *do* something to get it back and that she can do that on her own. She may discover that a ball will roll if she kicks it.

Learning through Play

Between the ages of 18 months and 24 months, if you have repeatedly pointed out your toddler's toe, nose, ear, etc., she should be able to point them out herself when asked. She should be able to fashion two to four blocks into a tower. She may try to feed her doll or stuffed animal. She should be able to identify pictures of objects that she has seen on a regular basis. During this time, almost anything around your house can be used for fun and to teach cause and effect. Let your child play in the tub by giving her cups, sponges, and other objects, and she will begin to learn all the fun things she can make happen in water. Provide a variety of toys for her to play with in a sandbox so she begins understanding what happens when she puts the sand in a bucket and turns the bucket over. Modeling clay is another great material for your toddler to squeeze, pull, and play with. These activities help her to realize that she has some control over the things in her world and can manipulate them to her liking.

Imagination and Imitation

It is not too early to introduce toys that can stimulate the imagination. Such toys include dolls, stuffed animals, play telephones, blocks, and trucks or cars. Foam-board puzzles are a great way for a child to begin learning to manipulate objects and to improve fine motor skills. Although it can be extremely frustrating for you, one of the most fun things a child can do to stimulate her imagination and creativity is to "play a song for you" with a kitchen pot and a wooden spoon. You know what comes next—wild, clanging, excited noise both from the object *and* your toddler's mouth! This activity may give you a headache, but it is providing your child with new ways of thinking and growing.

Imaginative play is just as much fun as imitative play. Your child will love wearing a cowboy hat, a ballet tutu, or just about anything else that allows her to play make-believe. This actually helps her to understand what other people are doing in her world.

The mirror is a simple, fun object to use for teaching imitative play. Toddlers love to look at themselves. Stick

You've probably heard the saying, "Imitation is the sincerest form of flattery." Well, get ready, because your toddler is going to begin using this new skill. Helping your child learn through imitation is an excellent way to help her start understanding the relationships between objects and their uses. Most of what she learns will be exciting for you to observe, but remember: she will imitate all sorts of things that you do, so you have to be careful!

your tongue out while looking in the mirror and encourage her to do it, too. When she sees herself doing it, she'll try it over and over again, much to her delight.

Finger puppets or hand puppets are another great way to encourage interactive play. Begin a story with your toddler in which each of you has a puppet and each of you has a role to play. Although she may not be able to completely verbalize what she is thinking, her actions and reactions will tell you that she is learning a great deal!

Toys

Finding out what your child is interested in is as easy as a trip to your local toy store. Take her along the aisles and pay attention to what strikes her fancy. Some toys will bore her quickly, but there will be others that she can't get enough of. Don't be surprised if your older toddler picks out toys that she liked as a 12-month-old. Between 12 months and 24 months, toddlers enjoy most of the same toys. Her tastes can change so that what she loved at 13 months will become the thing she doesn't like at all at 18 months. Then, out of nowhere, at 22 months, it will become her favorite toy again!

The following is a list of toys that you might consider having around the house for your toddler to explore.

- stacking toys
- push toys (cart, baby buggy, etc.)
- riding toys
- boxes, containers, and cups for filling and emptying
- toys that require an action, such as opening a door, pulling off the top, etc.
- stuffed animals
- dolls
- cars, trucks, trains, etc.
- modeling clay
- children's musical instruments

- a pretend lawn mower, vacuum, grocery cart, oven, or other "be like Mommy and Daddy" toy
- foam balls
- picture-books
- soft puzzles
- plastic blocks in shapes

Don't be concerned if your child seems to get bored easily with her toys or seems to enjoy playing with only a few items. When she gets bored, try introducing her to new games and activities, but only a few at a time. If she seems to be content with what she is doing, there is no need to overwhelm her.

The Importance of Play

To an adult, play just looks like play, but for a child, play is a critical way of learning about the world. Toddlerhood is the time to introduce books with pictures and puzzles with shapes. This type of play is most effective when you are sitting alongside your toddler. Look at each picture with her and identify what it shows ("This is a puppy dog, see?"). This will help her start assigning names and labels to objects. Take a crayon and draw a straight line on a piece of paper; then have your toddler do the same. Or pretend with her that the two of you are "cooking dinner." Until she sees you using an object, it may not interest her, or she may not understand why it even exists. Miniature versions of tools and appliances that you use around the house are great for developing this understanding as well.

Another skill that your toddler is learning as she approaches 24 months is the ability to sort and classify objects. For example, if you have a set of blocks that are in different shapes, you can try sorting them into two groups for her, such as circles and squares. It may take her a few tries, but she can begin learning to put them in different categories before she is able to name them verbally.

The most critical thing about learning through play during this period is that it must be as interactive as possible. Anything that requires participation and physical activity is interactive. Passive activities such as watching television or playing with battery-operated toys and even talking dolls should be limited. What you are trying to accomplish here is the development of imagination, creativity, and motor skills.

Fun Activities for Your Toddler

Here are some fun activities that you can do with your child. Aside from getting to spend some one-on-one time with her, you will also be improving her motor skills and imagination!

Play "find the shoe." Separate her shoes and have her help you match them back up.

- Give her a bucket of water, and the two of you can wash her toys outdoors. Get her a small broom and let her sweep while you are doing the same. You can also let her help you dust.
- Put on some music so the two of you can dance. Learn some songs that you can sing together.
- Have a ball toss with a foam ball and a basket or other container. Take turns throwing the ball into the basket.
- Take a spoon, cup, cookie cutters, and whatever you can think of outside with you and play in the grass!

First Words

Every parent looks forward to the day that his child says her first words. Even though you know it's coming, it's still a huge surprise when something pops out of your toddler's mouth.

Talking at 13 to 14 Months

By the end of your toddler's 13th or 14th month, she should be able to say "Mama" or "Dada." She should be able to follow verbal commands that require a single step. "Stop that," for example, is a single-step command. Telling her to stop what she is doing, pick up her shoes, and come to you is a multi-step task that will be beyond her. Make a habit of narrating your interactions with your child. For instance, when you hand her a glass of milk, say, "Here is your glass of milk." Every time your child hears the word "milk" or "glass," she begins to associate the words with the objects.

> **Understand that even though your toddler cannot yet *say* many words, she began to *understand* what words mean much earlier, especially if they are used regularly in your home.**

Talking at 16 to 18 Months

By about 16 months, your toddler should be able to use from 2 to 6 single words. Of course, just because she is using these words does not mean you can understand what she is saying! Still, she is making efforts to communicate, and you should listen to her carefully. By the end of 18 months, she should have the ability to name six simple body parts, such as "toe, nose, ear, etc." She should be able to use six words, although not necessarily at the same time. At this point, she should also be able to follow two-step commands. Now if you say, "Come here and sit down," she will understand and be able to perform—of course, that doesn't mean she'll choose to!

Talking at 18 to 20 Months

There is a big jump in vocabulary usage between 18 months and 20 months. By the end of 20 months, your child will have learned approximately 50 single words. She will be able to speak, but you still may only understand about half of what she says. Neverthe-less, you should encourage her to speak. Don't rescue her and say the words for her. By 22 months to 24 months, your toddler should be able to combine words to make short phrases or very short sentences. She'll be able to use prepositions, although not always correctly.

Helping Your Child Learn to Talk

As a parent, you can do a lot to teach your child to talk. Whenever possible, talk directly to your child. As you are getting her dressed, describe what you are doing. "Let's put on your shirt. Look at the buttons on your shirt. I like them, don't you? Now let's pull on your pants and zip them." Although it's obvious what you are doing and you may think it sounds silly, you are helping your toddler associate words with objects. If you see a cat curled in the yard as you are driving by, ask your child if she sees it. "Look at that furry cat. Do you see her lying there in the sun? She's taking a nap."

> Picture-books are another great way to teach your child new words. You can read the book, describe the pictures, and help your child point out what she sees. Later your toddler can begin doing it for her-self even if the words don't sound quite right!

At this stage, your toddler is not going to pronounce much of anything correctly. If you expect her to, you're going to be disappointed. Resist the urge to correct her. Toddlers really don't care how the word sounds, as long as they believe you know what they mean. With time, your toddler's speech will correct itself on its own. If you find that you simply cannot keep quiet when your child mispronounces a word, repeat the word in a sentence and then let it go. For instance, if she says the word "play," but it sounds like "pay," try saying, "I'll be happy to play with you." If she's listening, she will begin to pick up on the correct pronunciation.

Why Is My Child Scared?

All toddlers have fears. Some of them are very rational and reasonable, and others seem downright strange. Nevertheless, it is normal for a toddler to feel anxious and afraid when she encounters something new and unfamiliar. Unfortunately, until they are a little bit older, toddlers cannot express their fears with actual words. Therefore, it becomes very important for you to be a good observer so that you can watch for the signs that your child is becoming fearful or anxious.

> You don't want your toddler to be afraid of everything new she encounters, but you do want her to have "healthy fear," an age-appropriate wariness about things and situations.

One sign of fear is crying and whining upon exposure to something. Your toddler may draw away from the object as if she fears touching it. She may become overly clingy and grab onto you like glue! If there is ongoing stress in her life, such as a new sibling, she may start to have nightmares. If she is afraid of dogs, and the neighbors have gotten a new dog that barks ferociously every time you and your toddler are around it, it is bound to make her anxious and could cause bad dreams. You want to protect your toddler and make sure she is never scared, but this is not possible. Fear is part of the human survival mechanism, and it can actually be a good thing to guard against danger. You don't want your toddler to be afraid of everything new she encounters. On the other hand, being fearless is not necessarily healthy either. The fearless toddler does not anticipate danger and therefore will try anything, including things that are dangerous. You want your toddler to have "healthy fear," an age-appropriate wariness about things and situations. With a little comfort from you, she should be able to cope with her fears.

Helping Your Toddler Deal with Fear

What scares toddlers most? A dog, the dentist, the dark, the loud grocery-store clerk—just about anything has the potential to strike fear in a toddler, particularly if it is new, different, or something that they don't understand. The question then becomes not, "What scares my child the most?" but rather, "How can I help?"

First, remember that children's fears are often very real, although they may seem weird, silly, or out of proportion to you because you are an adult. If your toddler perceives something as a threat, it is real for her, and she will look to you to keep her safe.

Second, don't force her to "face her fears." Many parents think they are being helpful if they ignore their children's communications about being afraid and push them to "do it anyway." This will probably make the situation worse, and your toddler will become even more frightened. Also, she will begin to see you as unreliable and unpredictable when it comes to protecting her.

Third, don't make fun of your child and her fears. You may find it amusing that she is scared of her brother's pirate doll, particularly when he chases her with it. If it scares her, now is not the time to say, "He's only teasing you," or "Don't be such a baby." Even at their young age, toddlers can recognize your negativity and impatience. It's important for her to feel you have *heard* her and that you respect her feelings. Again, it's her perception that's important, and if she perceives something as dangerous, take her seriously.

Last, keep in mind that taking her fears seriously does not mean letting her fears run the household. In other words, the fact that your toddler is scared of the pirate doll does not mean her brother has to get rid of it. In handling fear with your child, you must communicate three things: (1) your understanding that she is afraid; (2) reassurance that she is safe; and (3) that although she is not in any danger, she does not have to face her fear.

Dealing with Fear: A Scenario

Let's look at the example of the neighbors' new puppy. It has a loud, fierce bark and sort of leaps at the gate when your toddler goes near it. Incidentally, the dog is wagging his tail the entire time and is known to be quite gentle. Your toddler doesn't know or care about that, though. She cannot tell you that she is scared in words, but she jumps and begins to cry when he starts barking. She runs to you and reaches her arms upward as if to say, "Pick me up and get me out of here!"

The wrong way to handle this would be to say, "Oh, he's just a puppy dog. There's nothing to be afraid of. He's just like Granny's dog. You're not afraid of Granny's dog." To add insult to injury, you then put your toddler down and grab her hand. You drag her over to the gate and put your hand out to the dog, which immediately stops barking and begins wagging his tail. Then you say something like, "See? He's not mean. Here, pat his head." Your toddler is likely to scream and run.

Instead, try picking her up and soothing her. Tell her, "You must be very afraid of the dog." As you remove her from the situation, you remind her, "You are safe here with Mommy. The dog won't hurt you, but you don't have to go over there." Using this approach almost always guarantees that her fears won't get further out of hand. As long as she realizes she is safe and that she can try again with the dog at another time, she is more likely to do so in her own time.

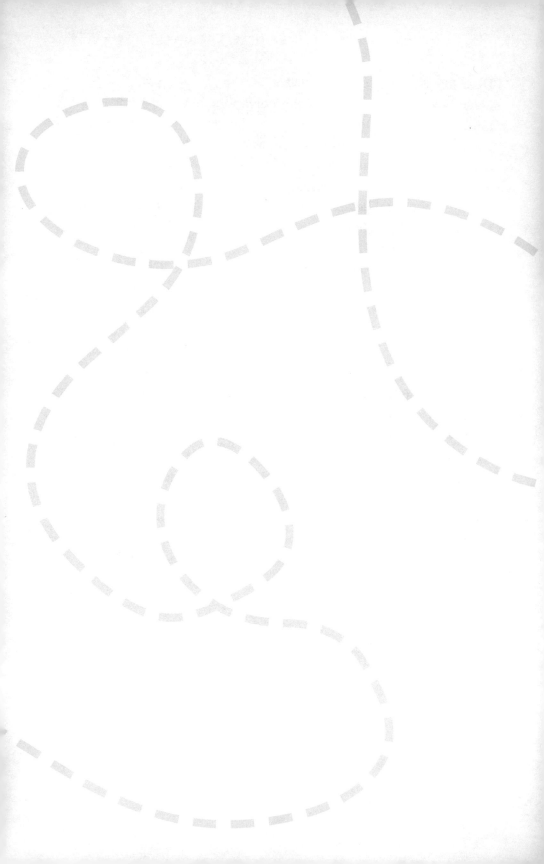

3

Emotional Development

First Signs of Separation Anxiety

There is good news and bad news about separation anxiety. The bad news is that almost every toddler will experience it to some extent or another. The good news is that it will eventually go away with a lot of help from you. Separation anxiety usually appears around the end of 12 months and can last until 24 months or even longer. It's hard to understand why some toddlers never have separation anxiety, but it is believed to be partly due to personality type and a less fearful attitude about change.

From the day he was born, your toddler has felt more secure and safe when he was with you or a consistent caregiver. Toddlers prefer predictability to separation. This is why, for example, some kids get very upset when they go to spend the night for the first time with their grandparents. Although they have been around their grandparents many times before, the separation from you triggers the anxiety, no matter how much fun he is told he will have in the new situation. Separation anxiety is thought to be more severe for children who are naturally more hesitant or shy. Also, if a new stress or change is introduced into his life, such as moving or the birth of a sibling, a toddler may react by becoming anxious.

Handling Separation Anxiety

Can you prevent separation anxiety from affecting your toddler? Sure, you can—if you decide to have no life away from your child! This is impossible, of course, but there are ways you can head off the anxiety or make it less uncomfortable for him. While you don't want to create separation anxiety that is not there, you do need to watch his behavior when you do something as simple as going to the bathroom and closing the door. If this is beginning to make him nervous, then it is time for you to take some preventive intervention.

The best way to handle separation anxiety is to start with short periods of separation.

Remember, when your toddler sees the person in front of him leave, in your toddler's mind, she's gone and she no longer exists. Try this: go into the bathroom, close the door, and wait a few seconds. If your child begins crying or becomes upset because he is not able to see you, open the door and reassure him that you're okay. Close the door again and see what happens. You can do this several times, but if he continues to get upset, he may not be ready to handle separation. If he does manage this without a lot of discomfort, try going into another room without him. If he follows you, don't discourage him. This may be another sign that he is not ready for you to leave him. If you get to the next room and he becomes anxious, yell out that you're in the next room or reenter the room where he is. If you have to leave to run errands, leave him with his other parent or a trusted caregiver. Make your absences very brief, working up to longer periods of separation.

Babysitters and Day Care

When it is time to leave your child with a babysitter or at day care, do not feel that you are causing him to suffer unnecessarily. Remember, separation is bound to happen sooner or later with your child, and you can't stick to him like glue until he goes to college! If you are planning to have a babysitter in your home, have the sitter over several times to play with your toddler while you're there. You might leave the room for a few minutes to see how your toddler handles your absence (and how the sitter handles him!). For your first trip out, run a quick errand and come back to see how they have done. If your toddler will be going to day care, take him several times if you can to visit but not to stay just yet. Introduce him to his teachers and let him get used to his surroundings. As his level of comfort and familiarity with the situation increases, he is apt to have less anxiety when you actually leave him there for the first time.

"Bye-bye" Routines

As you are getting ready to leave the house, keep your toddler busy doing something he enjoys. This takes the focus off of your preparations. If possible, spend a few minutes with him before you go. Read a book with him or have him pick out something he would like to do with you before you leave. This time with him is *not* for the purpose of telling him you are leaving. This extra attention should be focused on letting him know he is loved and helping him to feel secure.

When you're ready to walk out that door, be cheerful and as upbeat as possible. You may feel the need to have a long, drawn-out goodbye, but resist that urge. Instead, say, "I'm leaving now, but I'll be back soon. You and Sally will have lots of fun. Bye-bye." You might tell him that upon your arrival back home, the two of you will read his favorite book together, or go to get some ice cream. If you do this, however, be prepared to keep your word or this can backfire on you. As soon as you have said, "Bye-bye," simply leave. *Don't* pull the trick of leaving after your toddler has gone to bed. Although it might seem like you're doing him a favor, if he awakens and you're not there, he is likely to become even more anxious than before.

Feeling Guilty

Although separation can be very distressing for your toddler, it can be equally devastating for you. It's a horrible feeling to walk away from a child who is sobbing uncontrollably as if he's about to be tortured. If you are feeling guilty and anxious about leaving, your toddler will sense it. Remind yourself that it's okay for you to want or need some time away from your child, and actually, it's a healthy thing to do. The more relaxed and cheerful you can be about leaving, the more he will feel that it is okay for Mommy or Daddy to go. In addition, you don't want to reinforce the crying by returning to him, thinking that you can resolve the situation by hugging him, holding him, or deciding not to go. This will only make matters worse for your next departure.

> You can make separation between you and your toddler a game if he is ready. Rather than playing peek-a-boo in the traditional way, step behind a door or a piece of furniture. A watered-down version of hide-and-seek can help, too. When your toddler is able to giggle because he knows you are "right there," he may not find it as scary when you actually leave!

Taking Your Toddler Out

When you're planning to take your child to another location, such as his grandparents' house, consider two things. First, even though you know it's a treat, will your toddler feel that way? If he is going through a period of more difficult separation anxiety than usual, perhaps now is not the time to have a sleepover at Grandma's. Second, will the caregiver with whom your child is going to stay be able to handle your toddler's anxieties and insecurities? Although they may have the best of intentions, some caregivers simply cannot handle the crying, tantrums, and other troublesome behaviors that occur with separation anxiety. Although this caregiver may be perfectly fine at other times, you might want to consider other options for now.

Outgrowing the Fear

Please remember that separation anxiety *truly* does not last forever, although it certainly may feel like it will when you're in the midst of dealing with it. It's normal for your child to want to have you around all the time, but it's also normal for a toddler to want to experience independence. Let your toddler wander away from you when you are in a safe environment and welcome him back with open arms when he returns. When you leave, reassure him that you love him, and then you should wander away, too!

Your Toddler's Struggle for Control and Independence

Between the ages of about 18 months and 24 months, your toddler is changing rapidly day by day. One of the most frustrating things for a parent is when a toddler begins to exert some independence. The problem is not that a parent resents that her child wants to be independent, but that the behavior can be quite baffling! At one moment, your child may scream "No!" when you are trying to put on his coat. Five minutes later, he is motioning for you to help him put on the very same coat. He may wiggle out of your arms so that he can get on the floor and walk away from you, but just as quickly as he leaves, he wants to return to you and becomes clingy and whiny. Rest assured that your child is not merely manipulating you.

This is just part of the eternal struggle for toddlers—wanting to exert some independence over their own worlds, yet being fearful of it at the same time. His readiness to be independent is a good sign that he is developing healthfully.

Relating to Other Toddlers

Another obstacle your child will encounter on the road toward independence comes from the relationships he is beginning to have with other toddlers. These relationships are a necessary and important part of the socialization process, but they can still be very maddening for him. Because every child is different, there are bound to be vast differences in development among your toddler's peers. You are an adult, and you can understand this; but for a toddler, this is annoying. Your toddler cannot express in words that his friend John is driving him crazy because he cannot walk as far. Sharing and the ability to empathize with another person are skills your toddler has not mastered yet. Therefore, when both children want to play with the same toy, someone is going to come out on top. The one without the toy is apt to communicate his frustration by perhaps hitting or taking the toy away from his friend. Although any one of these interactions seems simple to a grown-up, these situations are opportunities for

Although your child's developing independence can be aggravating for you, consider your toddler's point of view. There are things that he wants to do on his own, so when you try to help him, he resists your attempts. However, he will also become quickly frustrated by the fact that he simply does not know how to do what he wants to do by himself. If you try to force your help on him when he is not ready for it, a toddler will do what a toddler does best—he simply will have no part of it!

your child to learn not only independence and control, but also to develop social skills.

How Independent Should Your Toddler Be?

So how lenient should you be in letting your child behave independently? Obviously, if he is doing something he is not allowed to do or something that puts him or others in danger, it is important to intervene immediately and correct him. In other matters, remember that toddlers are professionals when it comes to trying to take charge. Although your toddler may sense that you really don't want him to do something, he doesn't care about pleasing you; he would rather do what he wants to do. The more hardheaded you are about it, the more hardheaded he will become in the opposite direction! If you've ever watched a toddler who has been told to eat his sandwich, then you understand what this means. The more you tell him to sit in his chair and finish his sandwich before he can play, the more defiant he becomes. He may walk away, throw a tantrum, toss the sandwich across the room, or cry. However, if you leave him alone and pretend it is not bothering you, he is likely to come back to the food on his own and eat it without complaint.

Getting Your Toddler to Cooperate

If there is something you'd like your toddler to do, find a way to let him think he *chose* to do it himself. For example, if he is dawdling in the grocery store, your first reaction is likely to be one of frustration because it's taking so long to get your shopping done. Ask him, "Would you rather hold my hand or get in the cart?" Simple as it seems, he will typically choose one of the options, believing he did it "all by himself." If he is becoming increasingly frustrated because he cannot take a lid off a jar but resists your offer to help, pick up a jar and pretend to have a bit of trouble opening it, too. He will watch what you are doing and will either ask for help or learn from observing you.

Pick Your Battles

The most important thing you can learn about your toddler's growing independence and need for control is that you *have* to allow it to occur. Pick your battles. You do not want your toddler to feel stifled or think that he is constantly disappointing you because he's not doing things your way. You'll do well to develop a sense of humor and patience during this time and try to find the fascination that he also finds in his ability to do things on his own and learn from them. After all, he still needs you, but he also needs to see what he is capable of doing on his own.

Acting Out: What Biting, Scratching, and Hitting Really Mean

As you are beginning to understand, the world of a toddler can be both an exhilarating and annoying place! Because your toddler has not learned to express what he is dealing with through words, he communicates his emotions through his actions. For example, a hug means love, and a giggle expresses delight. Unfortunately, your toddler also has feelings of anger, frustration, and hostility. Biting, scratching, and hitting are means of expressing those feelings and other negative emotions.

Why Do Toddlers Hit?

Besides your toddler's inability to express emotion verbally, there are several other reasons for aggressive behavior. As your toddler is seeking to exert control over his little world, he is aware that many things cause him to be helpless. In an effort to fend off "threats" to his world, he is going to react out of a perceived need to survive. In addition, for a toddler, it is still "all about me." There is no real ability to empathize or "put himself in another's shoes." Although your child is trying to be independent, he lacks self-control at this age, so when he is frustrated, he acts without thinking about what the consequences will be.

When and How to Stop It

Not all hitting or pushing is bad. Because toddlers aren't capable of saying what they feel, most of them will engage in these behaviors at one point or another. Intervene when the argument appears to be escalating. When your child is the aggressor, and particularly if he is biting, you need to intervene immediately. Without yelling or becoming angry, you should firmly stop the behavior and show sympathy for the victim. This communicates to your toddler that he has hurt someone and that your attention is on that child. Only after you have comforted that child should you return to your own child. Look him in the eye, keep it simple, and state with confidence, "I know you're angry, but we do not bite (scratch, hit, etc.)." What you're trying to get across to your toddler is that it's perfectly normal to feel angry or hurt when someone won't give him a toy or won't play with him, but that aggressive behavior is not the answer to resolving the problem. Don't bother trying to give a lengthy explanation as to why his behavior is unacceptable. A toddler can't focus for that long, and your lecture will only frustrate him more.

> Parents often want to take sides when their children engage in these behaviors. You'll be better off remaining neutral so that the real message that the behavior is unacceptable gets through, rather than your own feelings about what has just happened. Instead of getting embroiled in the argument yourself, suggest that the kids switch to a different activity. Toddlers are quite forgiving of one another and will usually get back to being the best of friends within minutes.

Preventing Aggressive Behavior

Fortunately, there are a number of ways to help prevent aggressive behavior. First, take every opportunity to teach the lesson *before* your child is in the middle of an angry situation. For example, when you are reading a book where a situation was resolved appropriately, comment about it. Tell your child that the solution presented in the book was far better than hitting, biting, or scratching. If your toddler handles a particularly frustrating situation without engaging in these behaviors, praise him by saying, "I'll bet you were angry when John took away your truck. I'm so proud of you for not hurting John."

If you sense that your child is becoming angry, sometimes the best thing to do is to simply take him out of the situation. If it's close to nap time, for example, and your toddler is tired and cranky, he is more likely to act on his negative feelings. There's no reason to set him up for a possibly nasty confrontation with his friend. Help him to begin labeling his feelings instead so that he has an alternative to acting out.

Bite Back?

Should you bite back if your child bites you? The answer is an emphatic "No!" Nothing brings out the immature toddler side of a grown-up like a toddler! Resist the temptation to show your toddler how biting or hitting feels. He might be frightened temporarily if you bite back, but it won't last. Remember, a toddler's ability to understand that he has truly hurt someone is not that great.

What Those Cries Really Mean

For a toddler between the ages of 12 months to 15 months, crying is the primary means of communicating. Although your toddler may know several words, it's a little too early to expect him to be able to express himself verbally. Instead, toddlers have all types of cries: the hungry cry, the frustrated cry, the sad cry, the scared cry, etc. Parents tend to worry that they are missing the message behind their children's cries and that they are somehow damaging them for life. As long as you attend to your child you won't be causing long-term damage, but it becomes important as he is aging to understand what he is trying to say.

Is it Crying or Just Whining?

Equally frustrating at this stage is the difficulty for parents of differentiating between real cries of need and whining. Whining is crying that a toddler uses to get him what he wants because he has learned that his parents cannot stand to see him upset. There's hardly a parent out there who hasn't given into that sort of crying just to have some peace and quiet. Once this happens too often, however, the wrong message starts being sent to your child. Once your toddler knows that whining gets your attention and that it is likely to get him what he wants, he will whine every time he isn't getting what he's asking for. If your child is whining out of a real need, such as fear, you should help him try to label his emotion. If you know that your toddler is whining simply because you have denied him something, one of the best techniques is to ignore him. Your toddler is smart. Part of the game is to get attention because even negative attention is better than no attention at all! When you refuse to play along, the game loses its allure for the toddler. If you feel you cannot ignore this behavior entirely, try telling your toddler that you understand that he is upset and that when he stops whining, you will figure out how to solve the problem. But, after you do this, you must be prepared to ignore him and let him think about it.

> **The most important thing you need to remember about whining is that it's only as effective as your reaction to it.**

As your child reaches 15 months to 18 months of age, he is capable of using more words. Try helping him to label simple emotions. When you know that he is particularly tired, angry, or scared, respond with, "You must be feeling angry right now. Let's see what we can do about it together." He won't get it at first and will continue to cry and whine. Over time, however, if you employ this technique, he will start learning to communicate his feelings verbally.

Tantrums

Between the ages of 18 months and 24 months, and often beyond that, your child may start having tantrums. Tantrums are ugly, scary, and can cause even the most in-control parents to completely lose it. At times, your child may become angry or defiant or stomp his feet and scream, but this doesn't necessarily mean he's having a tantrum. This may be whining behavior that has accelerated so he can get what he wants.

A tantrum is something quite different. When your child is having a tantrum, he has simply lost control. Tantrums occur when whatever frustrations or other stressors he is experiencing grow too large for him to manage. Whatever coping skills he may have developed up until now are far outweighed by what he is feeling. He is trying to tell you that he can no longer "hold it together."

Handling Tantrums

How can you handle a tantrum so that your child is able to "let it out" and get some relief? First, you need to understand that you cannot argue, reason, or talk your child out of a tantrum. It is useless to try, and you both are likely to become even more frustrated. Your toddler is already upset, so your demands that he "cut it out" won't mean anything. If your child is not in physical danger, it is best to let him finish his tantrum. It is agonizing to watch, not only because it annoys you, but also because it upsets you to see him this way. If you can let your toddler have his tantrum in his own time, it is likely to end more quickly than if you intervene.

Tantrums in Public

First, the best thing to do when you are out with your toddler is to try to prevent potential tantrums from occurring. Again, if you know your child is hungry, cranky, or is exceptionally frustrated at that moment, you may need to take him home where he can cool down. If this is not possible, resist trying to threaten him by saying such things as, "If you make a scene, you'll be in real trouble." A toddler only understands this marginally, and as with most other toddler behaviors, he is likely to go ahead and see if you really mean it!

Pick your battles. For example, every child who can see the merchandise on store shelves wants something, or many things! If your toddler is already at risk for losing control completely, why would you pick this time to teach him that "You can't have everything you want."? There will be plenty of opportunities to teach him that lesson when he is in a calmer mood. Instead, gently tell him that you know he is tired, hungry, etc., and that he will be allowed to pick out one thing at the checkout counter when you are done shopping. You might engage him in a game of "What do you think you'd like?" You are *not* bribing him. Sometimes it's just not that important to deny him something for misbehaving.

If all else fails and a tantrum begins, the smartest thing to do is to pick up your toddler and physically remove him from the situation. Leaving him in the aisle to cry it out will only be embarrassing for both of you, and it won't resolve anything. When your toddler is out of control and needs to be taken care of, it is your job to see that this happens.

Is It Really a Tantrum?

A word of caution about tantrums: don't confuse your child's manipulations or expressions of displeasure with a real tantrum.

If a child stops in the store and begins to cry because you told him he could not have a toy, he may simply be trying to tell you that he is angry with you. He may think that if he cries loudly enough, you'll buy him something just to get him to be quiet! Only you can determine when your child's emotions cross the line into tantrums.

Part Two

The Trying Twos
(24–36 Months)

Hey, Look at Me!

Two years have already gone by, and unless you have completely passed out due to sheer exhaustion, you've no doubt had an incredible time with your toddler. Every time you turn around, he is learning something new. Toddlers see the world as no one else can. Seeing those experiences through his eyes is pretty amazing!

This stage in a toddler's development is often labeled the "terrible twos." You can't get around the fact that a lot of things that your toddler puts himself—and you—through will, in fact, be terrible! But "terrible" feels negative and quite foreboding; "trying" is a bit more optimistic. Actually, as he becomes more "trying," it is a sign that he is developing normally. He is growing, changing, and pushing his own limits, not to mention yours! He is going to make mistakes and will need your guidance more than ever.

Your best option is to keep, or find, your sense of humor and dive right in alongside him. Enjoy this time because, just like the last two years, they will pass in the blink of an eye!

4

Physical Changes

Walking, Climbing, and Other New Tricks

By now, your toddler is probably walking, running, and perhaps even climbing. Don't worry if your toddler is not doing these things; just remember that development happens on an individual basis and no two children are alike. Your friend's toddler who is the same age as your child may be running and climbing nonstop, but your child may have shown little interest in more than walking. Maybe he's not ready to go faster; his skills will develop as he becomes ready to face his fears. Perhaps you have carried your toddler a lot, and he has become used to having his own personal taxi service! *Do not* compare your child to another child, although the temptation is great. If you cannot shake your worry that there is a problem or that your toddler's skills are significantly delayed, consult your physician. Until then, try not to worry—your toddler will get moving when he is good and ready!

Skills at 24 Months

At 24 months, your toddler may have figured out how to remove an article of clothing, but he may not necessarily know how to put it back on. This becomes a great game for him when he realizes how much he can do all by himself. If he is already running, he may attempt to throw things, perhaps much to your dismay.

Skills at 25 to 33 Months

Between 25 to 30 months, your toddler will probably show interest in washing and drying his hands, and now he might also be able to put a piece of clothing *on*. If your toddler is especially coordinated, he may be able to balance on one of his feet for a couple of seconds and climb without taking so many spills. As he reaches 33 months, he may be able to brush his teeth with your help and should be able to put on an article of clothing such as a T-shirt. His balance should be improving, and you can notice this by watching him balance from one foot to the other.

During this time, you may as well find some activities that will allow your little climber to reach new heights while avoiding the things you'd rather he stay away from!

Skills at 36 Months

At 36 months, your toddler should have mastered balancing on each foot, but only for a few seconds. He may notice that he can jump with both of his feet. He may be able to dress himself without much help. Buttons, zippers, and laces might still be hard to figure out, however, and he is likely to put his shirt on backwards, but he *is* trying!

Climbing

Whether you are ready for it or not, climbing is a normal part of development, and there is not much you can do to stop it. Between the ages of 24 months and 36 months, the toddler is not nearly as clumsy as he was a few months earlier when climbing stairs was a dangerous feat. By now, he has fully learned the importance of using both his hands and feet to get on top of things, get around them, and to be the master of his universe! Your job is to encourage his curiosity while making sure that he is safe. Although all kids love to climb, some do it more than others. Provide as many opportunities for him to climb as you can. This is a good time to consider a backyard swing set or build a tree house that is very low to the ground (about 2 feet from it). If you live in an environment that has little space, such as an apartment, take him to the park where he can joyfully climb to his heart's content without having to be told to "stay off the furniture." If a park is not convenient, there are small jungle gyms available that you can put in a room for him to climb. There may be no space for your beloved piano, but he will be able to climb!

Coordination and Balance

If your toddler needs help with coordination and balance, the easiest way to teach these skills is to make them fun. For instance, throw a ball with him. (You might want to use a foam ball to avoid any injury.) He will start imitating how you throw and will get better and better as he practices. Try playing "hop." Jump from one foot to the other and encourage him to do the same. Depending on how coordinated he is, you might have to start by holding his hands while you do this. Sing or make up a funny story as you go along. Remember, toddlers are much more likely to do what you want them to do if they're having fun!

Working with Your Child's Sleeping Patterns

Between 24 months and 36 months, your toddler is likely still sleeping about 10 to 12 hours a day. By 36 months, most toddlers have given up one of their naps. Still others have given them both up. If this is the case with your child, you can expect your toddler to become grumpy during those times when he used to take naps.

Once he gets used to having less sleep, this crabbiness should disappear. If it doesn't, try changing the time your child goes to bed at night. If you are thinking that you can force your child to take a nap, forget it. This will only result in frustration for both you and your toddler.

Bedtime should be a pleasant time for your toddler. Resist sending your child to her bed for punishment. Do not threaten your toddler with sending her to bed early if she misbehaves. She will learn to think that going to bed is something unpleasant and thus will try to avoid it.

Nightmares and Night Terrors

Is there a difference between nightmares and night terrors? Yes, and learning to distinguish between them will help you know how to help your toddler. Nightmares are much more common than night terrors. Nightmares typically occur during the second half of your toddler's sleep. She will have a dream that is scary, but she will sleep through it. The fear doesn't begin until she is truly awake. Then she may begin to cry, panic, and beg for you. During a night terror, the child is not typically awake. She may appear to be wide awake, but you won't be able to "get through" to her. For example, you may be saying, "Mommy's here," but she will not realize it and instead will keep asking for you. She will not become fully awake unless you try to rouse her.

Your efforts to soothe your child during a night terror may seem futile to you for the most part. She may appear to be ignoring you or may even scream at you to leave her alone, which can be quite frightening to you. The best thing you can do is to let her finish the night terror while repeating to her that "everything is alright." Most toddlers recover much better than their parents do from night terrors. Children do not usually remember having these experiences, but the vision is likely to stay with you for quite a while.

Sleepwalking

If your toddler roams at night or sleepwalks, she will usually come to your bed. If she is successful, do not try to talk to her or fuss at her for not staying in her bed. She is not doing this on purpose—she is asleep! Gently guide her back to bed. An alternative is to put a baby gate across her bedroom door, but the chances are pretty good that she will only climb it or become more frustrated. Most toddlers outgrow walking in their sleep, so it is best to go along with it if you can.

Toddler Mornings

If your toddler wakes earlier than the rest of the family, you may begin to hear her talking to herself or her toys or stuffed animals in the bed. As long as she is content, leave her alone. This is a sign that she is learning to play by herself and that she is able to soothe herself to a degree. You might put some toys beside her bed that she is allowed to have when she wakes in the mornings. If she is crying for you, it is more than likely a sign that she is wet, hungry, or just downright frustrated that everyone else is still asleep! By 36 months, your toddler will learn to condition herself to hear your alarm clock or some other sign that it is time to get up and begin the day.

> **By 36 months, your toddler will learn to condition herself to hear your alarm clock or some other sign that it is time to get up and begin the day.**

The Family Bed

There is a lot of controversy about the "family bed"—whether or not you should let your toddler sleep with you. There can be nothing more fun than piling up in the bed with your toddler to cuddle and sleep. There's the added benefit that you are already present when your toddler wakes in the night. However, you should consider some of the problems that can occur when you regularly allow your toddler to sleep with you. There's the comfort aspect; too many bodies in one bed can be extremely uncomfortable, and, as a result, somebody is bound to lose sleep. Also, research shows that toddlers who sleep with their parents have a hard time separating themselves from their parents; this can interfere with the development of their independence and possibly make separation anxiety worse.

The Sloppy Eater

Eating can be a frustrating but fun time for the 24- to 36-month-old child. By now, he is no doubt eating more "grown-up" food, and he likely prefers to eat it when, where, and however he pleases. The parent who gets caught up in this eating game with a child is going to lose hands down.

Trying New Foods

Parents often think that this is the perfect age to start making their children eat certain foods. You can try all you want, but if they don't like liver and onions, they're not going to eat it! The more you pressure a child to eat certain foods and to disregard others, the more resistance you will get. We've all seen the dietary charts of what makes up a healthy diet. It is fine for you to try to add some of those foods into your toddler's meals; however, if she insists on having macaroni and cheese three times a day, that's okay too. You can always offer a bite of food that is new and different to your toddler, but don't become frustrated if she

> If a child has not been taught to equate food with punishment, a bribe, or as a reward, he is naturally going to see eating as a pleasurable experience. The trick is in *keeping* this experience a happy one.

refuses to try it. Children eventually will learn to incorporate other foods into their diets, just don't expect it to happen right away.

Nutrition and Healthy Eating

If you have serious concerns that your toddler isn't getting the appropriate nutrients, you can always add a multivitamin to her diet. Make sure, though, that it's a vitamin formulated especially for little ones. There are several good ones on the market. Ask the pharmacist or your pediatrician if you are unsure of which one to buy.

Remember that your toddler is a growing and very active little being. She may eat her dinner and then, an hour later, insist that she's hungry again. If she seems truly hungry, offer her a snack. But make sure that she's not eating because she is bored or tired. The last thing you want is for your toddler to start eating out of habit. This child will begin to want every cookie in the supermarket, or ask for a piece of candy when she is cranky. Not only will you be contributing to unhealthy eating habits, you'll also be sending your child the message that food is a great medication for emotions. Instead, encourage her to eat when she is hungry, and make eating an enjoyable experience for her.

Table Manners

If you're worried that your toddler is an extremely sloppy eater, take comfort in knowing you're not alone. All toddlers are messy, but it doesn't have to be the end of the world. Whether a toddler is eating with her hands, spoon, or something else, at least she is eating! If you feel your toddler needs to develop more appropriate table manners, you will need to model good table manners yourself. Don't expect her to pick them up right away, however. Toddlers don't learn by long lectures about how "you must put your napkin in your lap because that's what ladies do." They learn by imitation. Allow her to eat on the same dishes as everyone else. Of course, you may lose a few plates or have to watch her carefully, but a child is not going to learn to take care of nice things if she eats only on plastic. Even though many of today's families are always in a rush, at least once or twice a week you should try to find a time when you can all eat together. Family mealtime is an important opportunity for family bonding, and a great time to model table manners for your child.

Junk Food

Is it all right for your child to have junk food? Although we would rather our children eat healthfully 99 percent of the time, we must be honest and take a look at ourselves. We are a nation of fast-food eaters; we often snack and sometimes get by without meals at all. Your toddler learns her first eating habits from her family; but no matter how much you avoid the drive-through, your toddler may eventually be introduced to fast food. It is better to introduce these foods along with healthy eating habits. In this way, your child learns that junk food is not a substitute for healthy food, but that it is another option that your family may sometime choose. Unless you're going to be living in a cave with your toddler, there will likely be issues with junk food, and you need to tackle them early. Try not to let junk food become a habit, a bribe, or a reward for good behavior.

Mastering the Potty

Every parent is pleased when their toddler finally begins potty training. Unfortunately, however, you don't get to pick the time—your toddler does. Whether your toddler shows signs of wanting to use the toilet at 15 months or 28 months doesn't really matter. Research shows that most children can stay dry throughout the day by the time they are 3 years old. Starting your toddler's potty training too soon will only lead to frustration, anger, and a very resistant child. The time to begin encouraging toilet training is when your child seems aware that she is about to have a bowel movement or produce some urine. If, as a younger toddler, she concentrated, gritted her teeth, and became very red in the face while having a bowel movement, you should now look for the same behavior. In addition, however, you should look for some new behaviors that show she is anticipating the activity. She may hold herself or she may begin to look in her diaper to see what is getting ready to happen. These are signs that she's becoming aware.

Potty or Toilet?

There is much debate about whether to toilet train a child on a miniature potty or on a regular-sized toilet. It really doesn't matter, and you can leave it up to your toddler's discretion. Some children would rather imitate you and go directly to the adult-sized toilet. If this happens, you'll need to get a stool so that she can comfortably climb up onto the toilet. Other children like the small potty because it gives them a sense of control, and they are usually bigger than it is. When you know that your child is ready to use it, show her what happens when urine or feces goes into the potty, and tell her that when she is ready, she can use it. If she has the small potty chair, you can place it anywhere, but the best bet is to place it in a corner, somewhere in your own bathroom or her bedroom.

Learning and Accidents

Although your toddler is beginning to anticipate the production of urine or a bowel movement, she doesn't always have time to act on that feeling before she has an accident. If you know that your child has bowel movements at certain times of the day, you might watch her carefully, and when she appears to be preparing for a bowel movement, lead her to her potty. If she refuses to use it, do not become frustrated. At least she is now starting to get the idea that there is a connection between the two activities. It is also perfectly appropriate that your daughter go to the bathroom with her mother or your son with his father. Again, toddlers learn through imitation, and this is an excellent way to introduce what the toilet is being used for.

Potty Training Setbacks

As your toddler reaches 34 months to 36 months, she may be having fewer accidents, but she won't be perfect. With each success, praise her, but try not to blow accidents out of proportion. Remember, this is how we all learn. Becoming frustrated and angry is not going to do anything other than make your toddler more resistant to trying again. When there is an accident, tell your child that everyone has accidents, and that she will eventually get the knack of it.

Some toddlers dig their feet in the sand and have accidents "on purpose." This does not mean that your toddler is thinking about how to get back at you because she is angry and knows that this will irritate you. Bodily functions are one of the very few things a toddler can control. Thus, having an "accident" is a great way to feel like she's the boss!

As with everything else, there are going to be some setbacks during toilet training. If your child is staying dry pretty much all day but suddenly starts having accidents, it is a signal that something has changed in the child's life. She may be under more stress than usual. Examine her environment and determine if this is so. The stressor could be the introduction of a new sibling, the first time going on an overnight trip, or a problem at preschool. A child who is anxious is going to have accidents. Other children will just be so busy playing and having fun that they won't notice the urge to use the bathroom until it's too late. Again, the smart reaction is to respond cheerfully and not get angry.

Making Potty Training a *Positive* Experience

Whatever you do, approach toilet training as a positive experience rather than one that is looked upon with dread and frustration. You're trying to help a little child learn to master her body, and that's not an easy feat. If you can keep your aggravation and expectations in check, your toddler will show you what she needs to get the job done. Making fun of an accident or allowing your toddler to overhear you discussing her toilet-training mishaps is quite embarrassing for her and can actually hurt her self-esteem.

To make this period a bit easier, become the "potty police." Know where the nearest bathroom is wherever you go so that when your toddler announces she is ready, you spare no time in getting her there. Above all, remember that this is not *your* achievement; it is your toddler's. You are not a bad parent if your child is not toilet trained by a certain age. On the flip side, you're not a good parent simply because your child is completely toilet trained before everyone else's child. It is not a race. Your toddler will set the schedule, and if you really want to help her, follow her lead.

Noticing Gender Differences

How fun it is to discover something new and different about yourself! For a toddler between 24 months and 36 months, nothing is quite as fascinating as the discovery of a penis or vagina. The first curiosity usually comes when your child sees you or another child naked. This is when the questions begin.

If your child has seen you naked, he might not be as curious about himself or others. But there *will* be a time where he will ask you what "that" is. You need not explain its function because he simply doesn't need that much information and doesn't care. There is no reason for either of you to be ashamed, embarrassed, or anxious about these questions.

Talking About Private Parts

You may be wondering what you should call "it." That's entirely up to you. There's nothing wrong with calling a penis a "pee-pee," or a vagina a "too-too." Eventually, however, you will need to give your toddler the correct name. Some experts suggest using the real words as soon as toddlers start asking. Their reasoning is that it is nothing more than another body part, and we don't nickname our elbows, feet, or other body parts. Whatever method you choose, you cannot go wrong as long as you approach the topic with confidence and nonchalance. If you make a big deal of it, your toddler will, too.

A Note For Parents with Sons

Here's a word of advice for all of you who have sons. It is not a question of if, but when—your toddler *is* going to get an erection. What should you do? When this happens, resist the urge to giggle or become embarrassed. It's time for a direct approach. Your toddler is not having an erection because he wants a reaction out of you—it's just interesting! If he says, "Look what I can do!," calmly explain that you are aware that boys can sometimes make their penises big by touching them. It's not too early to begin explaining "good touches" and "bad touches" to your toddler. You may want to use this as an opportunity to explain what private parts are and who is allowed to touch them.

Playing Doctor

Remember, all your toddler really understands is that he's "got one." He has no clue that there is anything wrong with comparing his with a friend's. If you interrupt your toddler "playing doctor" with a friend, take a deep breath before reacting. Neither child needs to be shamed, embarrassed, or made to feel as if something bad has occurred. Simply mention that you see they are looking at each other's bodies. You may say, "I see you have a penis, and so does John." If you can't muster the courage to say that, then don't.

It's actually best to say as little as possible at such a moment. But you *do* need to stress to both of them that their private parts are just that—private—and that no one else needs to see them or touch them. Then, just as casually as you entered the room, help them get dressed and move on to another activity.

The less freaked out you are about your child's questions and behaviors in this area, the more quickly your toddler will lose his fascination. Usually, if you react to something strongly, it is going to seem forbidden and naughty. We all know it is hard to resist being naughty at times! You can't avoid this part of toddlerhood, and addressing it without drama will make your toddler feel that it's no big deal.

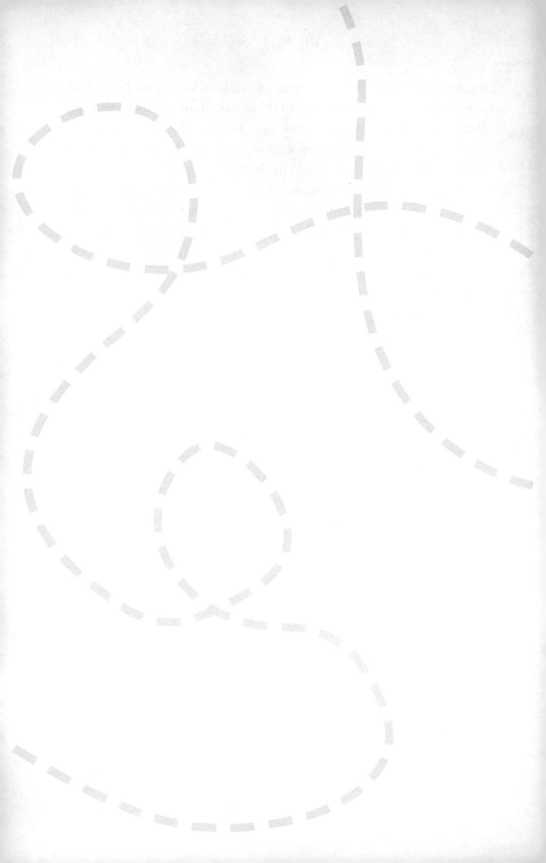

5

Cognitive Changes

Lessons Learned through Play

The stage between 24 months and 36 months is a wonderful time for children to learn through playing. They are able to refine their motor skills, perform elementary problem solving, and begin using their imaginations. When you realize that your toddler is learning all of this merely by playing, you begin to understand just how important play is.

Skills at 24 Months

At about 24 months, your toddler will be able to play with blocks and even stack approximately two to four on top of one another. She should be able to throw a ball over her head, and she can also jump up and down. She will be able to put on or remove an article of clothing, such as a sweater or T-shirt.

Skills at 28 Months

By 28 months, your toddler should be able to wash and dry her hands. Be sure that you have a stool available to her so that she can easily and safely reach the sink. There are new soaps on the market that make washing hands and brushing teeth much more interesting than the average bar of soap or tube of toothpaste. Having some of these available to your toddler will make this task more entertaining. Remember, if it's fun, she's more likely to do it. She should be able to brush her teeth primarily on her own, but she will still need your help. Get a toothbrush that is child-friendly and easy to use, and use toothpaste that is sparkly or special in some way for a touch of fun and enticement.

Your toddler is also learning to scribble at this point. This is not the time to try to convince her that she needs to draw a straight line or create a masterpiece. Instead, her individual imagination should be encouraged, and negative judgments or criticisms must be kept to yourself.

Skills at 30 Months

By 30 months, your toddler ought to be able to jump up and down, and she may even be able to make a broad jump. She should be able to put on one to two articles of clothing. This does not mean that she will necessarily put them on correctly, but she should be starting to make the effort. For her drawing at this age, she may be able to imitate you if you draw a line on a piece of paper and ask her to do the same. Her effort won't be as well formed as yours, but the important thing is that she is starting to adjust her fine motor skills to more detailed tasks.

Skills at 33 to 36 Months

Between the ages of 33 months and 36 months, your toddler should be able to complete a broad jump and should be able to balance on one foot or the other for a couple of seconds. She should be able to copy you if you draw a circle, a square, or a line on a piece of paper. Again, remember her performance will not be perfect. The idea is not accuracy but that she is showing curiosity about using these skills. She will be attempting to dress herself and can do so for the most part. However, her colors may not match, and she may put some things on backwards. This is not cause to worry.

Skills at 36 Months

By the age of 36 months your toddler should have mastered the ability to complete simple chores. For example, she should be able to take a food item from a bowl or container and put it on her plate. What you can absolutely expect is a surge in independence and an insistence to "do it myself." There is nothing wrong with this, and her independence ought to be encouraged as much as possible. Of course, this means that there will be much more of a mess for you to clean up, so you will have to be extremely patient during this time.

Helping Your Toddler Develop Motor Skills

All types of activities and objects are available to help a toddler develop her motor skills during this time. Keep games simple and noncompetitive. Remember that this is a time for learning, not winning. Buy some stickers and have her put a sticker next to a picture that matches it. Stickers are a great way to begin to learn colors, how to arrange or position items, and how to match items. Buy some chalk, crayons, and washable paints and let her go to town on paper. Music is

One of the most important thing to understand about play during this time is that it should be entertaining. If it's not fun, your toddler will become bored very quickly. The more dramatic the play is, the more your toddler is likely to learn from it. For example, when playing dress-up, you should react on a large scale to what she is doing. Try to respond with something like, "I see you have on your magic shoes. Show me all the things they can do." Toddlers love an overreaction that is positive and joyful.

an excellent way to introduce your child to dancing and learning rhythm. It also has the extra benefit of wearing a toddler out!

Many toys can help with motor-skill development during this time. Most toddlers, whether male or female, show some sort of interest in dolls. This is because a doll looks a lot like they do, and so a natural curiosity is formed. Dolls that require feeding, changing, or dressing are excellent for motor-skill development. Toys and activities that stimulate motor-skill development as well as imagination are ideal at this stage; they include dress-up clothes, toys that mimic adult activities (for example, lawn mower, toy oven, and tools), puppets, and puzzles that have different shapes and pictures on them. One of the best items for motor-skill development is modeling clay. Whether you make your own or buy it at the store, children are endlessly fascinated with the ability to mold, pull, stretch, and shape this substance. It's fun for grown-ups, too!

Messy Play

Toddler play is messy. Remember, toddlers are not born knowing how to be tidy creatures. They are more likely to spread all of their toys around them and then pick the one they wish to play with. If they are painting, they are going to be awkward and clumsy. The best thing to do is plan ahead. For example, spread a sheet underneath the paper if your child is painting on the kitchen table. Resist the urge to keep your toddler clean throughout these activities. Remember that you are trying to encourage the development of their motor skills and imagination, not their "clean-up" skills.

> **Above all, playing must be as physical as possible. The more your toddler must interact using her body and body movements, the more fun she is going to have, and the more her boundless energy will be used to her benefit.**

Stringing Words Together

Talk, talk, talk. By 24 months, your toddler has really begun to talk. He's expressing himself as quickly and enthusiastically as he can. At 24 months, he ought to be able to identify an item by naming it rather than pointing to it. Although you may not understand what he is saying, he may be attempting to string words together to make simple sentences. By 28 months, he may know approximately 50 words. He may not always know how to use them properly, or describe them to you, but he will be able to recognize the words. He is often able to identify someone by name who is not in the immediate family, such as a playmate or a caregiver. By 30 months, he may be able to name as many as 6 body parts, although he may not know what the body parts are used for. He may know one or two colors and may be able to tell you how several objects are used. Between the ages of 33 months and 36 months, your toddler may be able to count to three and will likely begin to have short "conversations" with you; that is, he can string two to three sentences together and maintain concentration long enough to interact with you. He may also know as many as four colors and the beginning of his ABCs.

"Why, Why, Why?"

Although this is an exciting time for a parent to observe and enjoy, the development of your toddler's speech may also be very frustrating and irritating. For instance, between the ages of 24 months and 36 months, the ever-popular "whys" begin. You tell your toddler to do something, and he will ask, "Why?" You may make a simple statement as you're driving down the street, such as, "That building looks like it was just painted," and your toddler will likely respond with, "Why?" Asking "why" is an important way for your child to gather information. Remember, everything in his world is new and changing every single day. "Why" is the child's way of figuring out how things work, what things are called, and how it all fits together. The "whys" will likely drive you crazy at many points. "Why" will become such a popular word in your toddler's vocabulary that you may start thinking it is the only word that he knows how to use! The other thing to remember about your toddler's "why" habit is its other purpose—getting attention from you!

Should you respond to every "why?" In the beginning, you should address every question with some sort of explanation if you can. If the question seems to be used excessively, your toddler might be trying to get you to pay attention to him. If this is the case, stop what you're doing, spend some time with him, and see if this helps reduce his ploys to get your attention.

Something else you may observe during this age is that your toddler begins to talk to himself—a lot! Do not fear. As toddlers begin to learn about the world and imitate others, there is an overwhelming desire to try all of their new skills. Toddlers do not discriminate. They will talk to anything. This is why you'll notice a toddler talking to the television, the dog, or a toy animal. You may also find him rambling on and on about nothing and to no one in particular. Do not discourage this because it will soon disappear as he becomes more proficient in communicating.

> **Above all, letting your toddler "do it himself" should be, for the most part, a successful venture. Make tasks as simple and straightforward as possible. Set the stage for success so that he continues to pursue his independence. No matter how aggravating it can be for you, you are helping him learn important communication skills and boosting his self-esteem at the same time.**

"I Can Do It Myself!"

How many times will you have to hear this? Remember that your toddler is learning new skills and striving for some autonomy. Just about everything he tries, he'll want to try on his own. Unless it's going to hurt him, there is no reason to deny him this opportunity. Of course, because he is learning, all tasks will take a lot longer than usual, and you will often find yourself running late *and* running out of patience. The best thing to do is to pad your schedule with a little extra time, knowing that some amount of dawdling is going to occur. Resist the urge to butt in and rescue your toddler if he is not able to succeed at a task initially. Obviously, as he becomes more frustrated, the need for you to step in and help will be important, but this does not mean you have to do the task for him. Rather, you might tell him, "Let's see how we can make putting your shoes on a little easier. Should we try this?" Offer options, not imperatives. This allows him to begin the important skill of talking through a problem and generating solutions.

A lot of children grow up in bilingual homes. Children can learn a second language a lot more quickly than adults, but between the ages of 24 months and 36 months, this is a lot of for your toddler to process. If possible, try to speak one language consistently with your toddler and introduce him to a second language later.

Concerns About Your Toddler's Speech Development

Parents may begin to worry if a child is not talking as much or as well as his peers. This is not the time to compare your child's language development skills. Many things influence the rate and depth of speech acquisition. First, remember that your toddler has only a finite amount of concentration. He may be using a good bit of it to focus on play, learning to jump and walk, for example.

There simply isn't always enough attention to go around, and if he is using his concentration to learn in one area, he may not be focusing on what he is saying or how to pronounce it. Second, toddlers who have older siblings often do not develop speech as quickly as their siblings did. This is probably because the siblings are doing most of the talking, and your toddler finds that there is no need for him to speak. In addition, if a toddler is trying to speak, and an older sibling or even a parent continually interrupts and finishes his sentences for him, he eventually learns that there is no need for him to ask for what he wants. Encourage your toddler to speak for himself and caution your older children to give them the opportunity to speak. As a parent, even though you may grow weary and impatient, try to let your toddler finish what he is saying without interrupting or rescuing him.

Stammering and Stuttering? Not to Worry.

If you find that your toddler is stammering or stuttering at this age, do not immediately assume that he has a speech problem. Often, children are thinking more quickly than their mouths will move. We've all had the experience of trying to say what we are thinking, but having our thoughts race so quickly that we can't get our words out fast enough. A toddler will say the same portion of a sentence over and over or trying to get a word out. Even though you may want to help, don't interrupt or put the words in his mouth. Let him figure it out for himself, and he will eventually develop a pace of speech that works for him.

Active Listening

As a parent, your job during this time is to *be present*. Ask questions, listen attentively, and interact with him. A toddler actually has the ability to realize that you aren't really listening to him, even though you may be saying, "Really?" or "Uh-huh." When your child figures out that you're not really engaged, he is likely to do something negative to get your attention. Therefore, it is important for you to actively listen. Look him in the eye, ask questions, and make remarks that indicate you really have been listening. Be the best dramatic audience for him that you can be because this will encourage him to talk further about everything!

First Responsibilities

When your child reaches the age of about 33 months to 36 months, she will continue to insist on doing things herself. Because this is a natural reaction for her, it is also a perfect time to begin teaching responsibility. A toddler at this age can handle small chores. Although she may not understand the importance of completing chores, she is likely to be a very excited and willing participant. Although giving her chores may help you accomplish some tasks that need completing, the important thing is that she is learning a great deal in the process. This is an excellent way to help her develop motor and verbal skills as well as to boost self-esteem. The completion of most chores may need your supervision, but not your participation.

Toddler-Sized Chores

There are thousands of different activities a child can do that will enhance her sense of accomplishment. These "chores" will not be done perfectly, so if you're expecting accuracy, your best bet is to do them yourself. Be sure you match the chore to your child's ability level as much as possible to prevent failure. Remember, chores at this age are meant to enhance self-esteem and a sense of mastery. If the chore is too frustrating, your toddler, who is easily irritated, will give up. Some frustration is appropriate, but if your toddler finds that she cannot complete a task, stop her and offer an alternative task. Although it is okay for you to help a little, this should be a last resort.

Here is a list of chores that your toddler may be able to carry out.

- Pick up her toys and put them in a basket
- Put her socks or other items of clothing in her drawer
- Carry a small trash can to the kitchen for emptying
- Dust and sweep
- Stir cookie dough, pancake batter, or other simple liquids for cooking
- Water plants, pull weeds, and plant seeds
- Carry a small sack of groceries from the car to the kitchen

Pushing Just Enough

Your middle name during this stage of your toddler's development should be "Patient." We all want our toddlers to learn, grow, and become successful adults. Pushing them too much or not enough leads to problems with self-esteem and the inability to mature from one stage to the next. Your toddler is likely to set the pace for just about every activity she encounters, and you may as well allow it. Hurrying her or suggesting that she slow down will only result in a stubborn refusal to do it your way. Stay patient and give yourself plenty of time for the task to take longer than you expected.

There are thousands of different activities a child can do that will enhance her sense of accomplishment. What you're striving for is to give your toddler as many chances for success as possible while keeping failures to a minimum.

6

Emotional Development

Tantrums and Crying

Of course, just when you think the tough times might be over, the difficulties associated with the "trying twos" continue to plague you and your toddler! By now you have learned what the causes of your toddler's tantrums might be and some ways to handle them. Here are some more techniques for handling those nasty moods.

Plan Ahead

Planning ahead cannot be emphasized enough. If you know that your toddler is prone to tantrums when he is hungry or tired, do not take him to a place where he cannot rest or get something to eat. Do not expect him to be on his best behavior at the supermarket when he has missed his nap. Working around your toddler's moods does not have to wreak havoc on your plans for the day if you work out the details ahead of time. Organize the errands, engagements, and other activities that you and your toddler will be doing together based on *his* schedule, not yours. Although you may feel that you are not getting a lot of things done efficiently in terms of time, you will save yourself and your toddler from exhausting, time-consuming tantrums.

Be Consistent

Whatever you do, try to keep your rules as constant and regular as possible. This will help you avoid unwittingly rewarding your toddler for a tantrum. For example, resist the urge to bribe your toddler when you go into the grocery store. We're all guilty of promising a piece of candy or a toy if a child can just sit still and quietly for 10 minutes. Although this may sound perfectly reasonable to you, it is very hard for a toddler to maintain behavior for longer than a couple of minutes. If he *is* able to hold out for his reward, you may be setting him up for a tantrum as he becomes more impatient and frustrated. The way that you decide to handle your toddler's tantrums should be consistent. For example, if you choose to let your toddler "cry it out," make sure that you at least try that technique whenever he has a tantrum. This gives your toddler certain expectations that he can rely on when he is out of control.

Holding Your Toddler

Some parents ask whether holding a toddler during his tantrum is appropriate. This is a great technique if your toddler is not sensitive to touch and will let someone soothe him when he is upset. If he is sensitive to touch, leave him alone and do not take it personally. Try to remove your toddler from the situation if possible; this will give him some space to deal with his emotions and to avoid being embarrassed.

Timeouts

Because timeouts work well with toddlers who are having tantrums, you might want to consider using them as a method for helping your toddler get himself under control; however, if you are going to do this, you cannot use timeouts for punishment. A toddler cannot understand the difference between a timeout that is meant to help him and a timeout that is meant to punish him. When your child begins his tantrum, simply say to him quietly, "I can see that you're getting frustrated. Let's take a walk together and get away from here." Say what you can to communicate to him that he is safe.

Why Is Your Toddler Crying?

Your toddler's crying patterns may continue to bother you. Even though you think you know your child well, as he ages and matures, his expression of emotions will change. Toddlers between the ages of 24 months and 36 months cry for five general reasons:

- fear
- frustration
- helplessness
- anger
- unhappiness

> Offer descriptive words to help your toddler label what his cries mean. As he becomes better at expressing his feelings verbally, he'll be less likely to resort to tantrums.

If you find that your toddler is crying more than usual or crying consistently at certain times or in certain situations, he is most likely trying to express his negative emotions. He may be afraid of something. The task that he is undertaking may be frustrating because he is not able to master it. He may feel a sense of helplessness, especially in new and different situations. He may be angry at one of his pals but not know how to assert himself. Or he may just be unhappy and dissatisfied with whatever is happening at the moment. As a parent, you can help by offering descriptive words to help him label what his cries mean. Doing so will help him to master verbalizing his emotions, and as he becomes more proficient at this, the crying should begin to subside.

Handling Individual Temperaments

By now, you have probably noticed that your toddler is developing his own personality. Some parents are perfectly happy with whatever personality their toddler has, whereas other parents are somewhat disappointed to find that a child has personality characteristics that they may not like. First, all parents need to understand that there are going to be things about their children that they may not like. Temperament is partly inherited and partly developed as a result of the environment in which a child thrives. This is why no two children are alike and why you can sometimes feel that your child is different than you. Other parents complain that they have certain traits of their own that they hope they do not pass on to their children, yet they begin to see those characteristics popping up quite early.

> You should understand that temperament is generally steady, and your toddler's personality characteristics are not going to change dramatically. This does not mean that you cannot help a child who has a bad temper to learn to control himself—you can. If your child is shy, there are ways that you can help him to be more comfortable around people. But the characteristics are there, and they're probably not going away.

Whatever your child's temperament, it is important that you accept your child for who he is and find ways to help him to be as healthy and happy as possible.

Accepting Your Child as He Is

Simply saying, "I accept you" is not enough. Truly accepting your child means really honoring your child's personality. It's important for you to lose the expectations that you had when you were holding your bundle of joy and envisioning his future. The sooner that you can do this, the sooner you will be able to let go of your disappointment and expectations. In turn, your toddler will begin to sense your acceptance, a key element in the development of his self-esteem.

You've probably heard a parent say to a child, "You're just like your father when you act that way!" Although this may sound innocent, a child hears this quite differently. Not only are you communicating that whatever he is doing is negative, but also that being like his father is not something he should strive for. Although you probably wanted to point out that your toddler's temper, for example, reminds you a lot of your husband, the words get twisted and misconstrued. Make an effort to curb the behaviors he uses to express anger, but take the emphasis off trying to change him.

It is natural and normal for parents to compare their children, and when your child's qualities fall short when compared with your other child, you may become disappointed and frustrated. No two children are alike, and the strengths inherent in one child may be the weaknesses that you observe in your other child. Rather than asking your toddler to be more like his older sister, look for ways to celebrate the siblings' differences. Help both siblings feel comfortable in their own skins and they will find a way to use their strengths and weaknesses positively.

Baffling Behaviors and Difficult Questions

No matter how well you know your child, there are all sorts of behaviors that are baffling, surprising, and often worrisome to you. Although an entire book could probably be devoted to this topic, the following is a discussion of some of the more common behaviors that your toddler might exhibit that might make you scratch your head and wonder.

Sensitivity to Touch

Some babies from birth do not like to be touched or held tightly, and some children are just more naturally resistant to touch than others. This can be devastating for a parent who longs to cuddle, kiss, and hold their child. However, if your toddler does not like to be touched, do not take it personally and worry that you have not bonded with him. Some children simply do not need as much physical attention as others. Others become resistant to touch for some reason only to return to their normal state of being. It's okay to attempt a hug even though your child may not like it. It's important to remember that this is not a personal rejection of you. Simply lessening the length of time you hug him may make your child more receptive. Still other toddlers may not be able to handle a tight embrace but will be perfectly willing to accept a quick hug or a pat on the shoulder. Whatever you do, find a way to express your affection for your toddler while respecting his need for close contact or extra space.

Toileting Accidents

At this age, some "accidents" can be related to stress, anger, concentration on play, or other reasons as discussed in Chapter Four. It's important for you to remember that he is, after all, a little toddler. It is perfectly natural to have accidents, and your best bet is to expect them during times of change and stress. The best way to handle these accidents is not to overreact or scold. Respond positively to his successes by celebrating, and respond to his accidents by helping him to accept them. Tell your child that it's perfectly normal to have an accident every now and then. Reinforce that it's no big deal. Doing so will prevent your toddler from using toileting accidents to get your attention or to express anger.

The "Outdoor Potty"

Many a parent has gone outside to find her toddler urinating someplace she would rather he didn't—in a bush, swimming pool, or fountain, just to name a few. Most are tempted to scoop the child up, scold him for using the bathroom outdoors, and tell him that it should never happen again. The bad news is that it probably *will* happen again. The good news is that he won't continue doing this for very long as he comes to realize that his peers are no longer doing it either. Sometimes a child urinates outside because he simply cannot wait to get indoors. When this happens, should you react negatively? After all, you're trying to teach him to use the bathroom rather than soiling his clothes. A toddler won't understand why it wasn't okay to go outdoors instead of soiling his pants. If this behavior occurs in public, bite your tongue and don't overreact. Simply let your toddler finish and then lead him quietly to another spot where you can explain to him that using the bathroom means going in a toilet. He will soon realize that this is an embarrassing thing to do in front of others and will probably stop on his own.

Shyness

Is your toddler shy or somewhat avoidant when around others? Your toddler's resistance to being around others is not necessarily about shyness; at this age, it's hard to tell whether this behavior is a personality characteristic or simply a reaction. It might be that he is a bit tentative around others and unsure about how to act. As a result, he becomes more clingy than usual and won't leave your side. Other children are shy because they do not know what to expect, which leads them to be wary of their surroundings and may cause

> **A word of warning about shyness. When a toddler is shy, a parent is usually quick to step in and talk for the child. Hold back if you can and let your toddler respond first, in her own time. If it becomes apparent that she is not going to do so, then you may step in and talk.**

them to be labeled shy. There is no reason to worry about it, but there are things you can do to help. First, accept that your child might be uncomfortable in certain situations. No matter how friendly and outgoing he may be, your toddler simply may not feel that way all the time. The more you push him to react in a way that you deem to be appropriate, the more likely he is to become withdrawn. Although it's okay to encourage him to engage in activities with other children, if he is steadfastly uncomfortable and adamant about not wanting to do so, you must honor this need. If you're convinced that this is truly a problem and that your toddler's shyness is causing him extreme discomfort and unhappiness, talk with your pediatrician about techniques that can be used to intervene and conquer shyness.

Not Following the Rules

A common lament among parents of children of any age is that their kids just don't follow the rules, but toddlers, in particular, seem to make it their job not to follow rules. Remember, they are developing their own autonomy and independence, so your rules will seem unnecessary and trite. Some of this resistance can be alleviated by doing several things.

Keep the rules simple and consistent. Although toddlers do have memories, they don't have long ones. Making a rule that is long, involved, and detailed will only result in noncompliance. If you must explain yourself, do so simply and quickly, avoiding a wordy conversation about the rules. A toddler can sense when you are not on top of your game. When you spend a lot of time explaining yourself, he will quickly realize that there is some wiggle room in which he might be able to manipulate you. Refrain from making too many rules. A toddler who feels confined and restricted is going to rebel. Having a long list of rules is asking for trouble.

Be willing to repeat yourself often. Many parents say they shouldn't have to repeat the rules because they have already listed them and their child should be listening. Wrong! Toddlers have a lot on their minds, and your rules are at the bottom of their priority list. Therefore, you should expect that you will have to repeat the rules often.

Pick your battles. Rules are meant to keep your toddler safe and to help her learn acceptable behavior. Rules are not meant to change her personality or to keep her from having a good time. Therefore, when you are making rules, try to keep them easy and view their compliance as a successful experience.

When the rules are followed, applaud and compliment your toddler. When the rules are not followed, first determine whether your rule is reasonable and easy and whether your toddler even understood it. Second, determine whether the noncompliance was voluntary or unconscious. Most toddlers are so busy doing other things that they don't really think about the rules. Your children are not perfect. The rules are not perfect. With a toddler, rules are a bit baffling. They're going to be broken much more than they will be followed. When some rules are broken, it might be because your toddler was too busy learning something else to follow the rule, or perhaps it was a little unreasonable to begin with. Even so, it gives you the opportunity to alter and change the rules as your child grows, and compliance will slowly increase.

If your toddler is particularly independent and somewhat defiant, she may take off her clothes as a way of getting your attention. This is something else that she can now control, and taking her clothes off is her way of showing you that she knows it. The best reaction you can have is no reaction at all. If this is occurring in public, it is important to quietly explain to her that there are certain places that nudity is not acceptable.

"Daddy (or Mommy), What Is That?"

Eventually your toddler is going to ask this sort of question. When your toddler was born, it seemed perfectly natural and completely normal to be nude in front of him. However, as he has gotten older, he has become more curious. When he sees you nude, he is apt to ask questions or make comments to others that you prefer he not make. There is no hard and fast rule as to when you should cover yourself in front of a child. However, most experts agree that the ages between 24 months and 36 months is the perfect time to begin do so. This is also a great time to introduce the notion of privacy and to explain that everyone's body needs to be respected. The discussion of "good touches" versus "bad touches" should begin now as well. Although you do not want to be overly uncomfortable regarding this topic, it is certainly appropriate to draw the line at some point.

Embarrassing Questions

"Where do babies come from? "Why is Grandma's face so wrinkly?" "Why is that man's tummy so big?" No matter what you do, you cannot stop your toddler from asking questions. In fact, a child who asks lots of questions is curious and wants to learn. With regard to questions about where babies come from, keep your discussion at an age-appropriate level. Even a 3-year-old can understand that mommy is growing a baby in her belly. There's no need to go into how it got there or what is going to happen when the baby is delivered. Most toddlers will accept a simple explanation, and that is really all they can handle anyway.

As discussed in Chapter Four, nothing is more exciting than realizing you have body parts that you can control by doing certain things to them. For example, it is natural for a boy to be fascinated with his penis. To your complete horror, he may want to show it to other people or will ask them if they have a penis. If this occurs, you can expect and understand that the person being asked might be caught off guard. No matter how funny or how embarrassing the questions might be, try to answer them straight-forwardly and with as little drama as possible. Try not to give a lot of attention to his comment, and he probably won't feel the need to ask it again. Remember that often your toddler is trying to get your attention, and he may find his questions funny, especially if you have laughed at them before.

Explaining Death to Your Toddler

The experts disagree about how the subject of death should be handled. One reason is that toddlers tend to develop a lot of irra-tional fears. Giving toddlers some understanding of death may con-tribute to their fears, so some experts suggest staying away from the subject. However, this is not the popular view. Most experts agree that death is part of life, and unfortunately, a toddler may lose someone he loves. Giving him no information about what happened to his grandma, for example, is not healthy. Handle death as you would other delicate matters—at an age-appropriate level. Try to reassure your toddler that, although the loved one will not being coming back, he is not suffering, and everything is going to be alright.

Sometimes a toddler develops a fear of losing a parent once a death has occurred in his little world. You need to confidently reassure him that you are not planning to die and that you will continue to be with him. Is this a lie? Yes and no. Remember, a toddler can only handle so much information. It will be up to you to decide how far to take this conversation.

Pointing Out Differences

We are all different, and tod-dlers are often the first to notice and make a comment about it. In his innocence, your child will think nothing of saying to you, "Look, Mommy, that lady has a big bottom." When he says this, of course, he will do it in his loudest voice (or at least that's how you'll hear it!), and the person about whom the comment was made will hear it, too! Although it is embarrassing for you and certainly for the person being commented upon, do not scold and insist that your toddler apologize. Toddlers are not usually malicious, so your child won't even realize he has said something hurtful; he is just saying what is on his mind.

In more quiet moments with your toddler, it is important to discuss people and their differences. He should understand that some people are large and some are small. Some are brown, some are white, and so forth. Whatever the differences may be, however, teach him respect for others. Help him see that although we may have varying characteristics, we are all "just people."

Understand, however, that you can't always prevent your toddler from asking questions at inopportune times. When it happens, stay calm and don't overreact. Quietly but sternly, try to direct the conversation to another topic. If that doesn't work, you can try taking your toddler away from the focus of his attention. If all else fails, whisper gently that you will answer him when you get to the car or leave the area.

Lying

Even if you are the very best parent in the whole world, your toddler *is* going to lie. The most obvious reason for lying is to avoid getting into trouble. Another reason is that your toddler may remember something differently from the way it actually happened. Although he sounds as if he is lying, he may be telling the story based on his faulty perceptions. Still others are not yet able to grasp the difference between lying and the truth. When your toddler tells his first lie, do not immediately assume he is headed down the road to a juvenile detention center! If you are modeling honest behavior and encouraging truth telling, your toddler is not likely to lie forever.

When a child lies about something he has done, it is best not to punish him or admonish him. Rather, explain to him that you know he did something and that it wasn't the right thing to do. If you yell and scream, you are merely setting up your toddler to lie the next time to avoid your wrath. If a child feels that it is actually okay to be honest, he is more likely to tell the truth. Backing your child into a corner by insisting that he's lying is only going to result in both of you becoming combative, angry, and frustrated. It's not a good idea to promise that if your child tells the truth, there will be no consequences. This is not reasonable. Do be sure to distinguish between what your child did to break the rules and his telling the truth about it. He needs to understand that the punishment is for the

> Fostering truth telling in a toddler can best be accomplished by making it a positive experience. When your child does tell the truth, compliment him and thank him for telling the truth. Explain to him that this makes you happy because telling the truth is very important.

behavior, not his honesty. The best thing to do is to tell your child that his behavior was unacceptable and that there will be consequences.

Nose Picking

If you got a nickel for every time you've had a reason to ask your toddler to stop picking her nose, you might be able to make a sizeable down payment on her college education! Whether you like it or not, all toddlers pick their noses. Some pick their noses because there's something in there, or at least they think there is. Others pick their noses because, as the old joke goes, it's sitting right there for the picking! She may be curious as to what is in there, or she just may be bored. Whatever the reason, most toddlers are fascinated by the gooey mucus that comes from their noses. If you just can't stand her nose picking, the best thing to do is to offer her another activity. Find something else that she can do with both hands that is constructive. Remember, toddlers are smart, and as soon as they know there is a way to test you, they are going to be off and running. The more you nag, scold, and pull her hand away from her nose, the more she is going to want to pick it. If possible, your best bet is to ignore what she is doing. Eventually she will find something else that piques her curiosity.

Refusing to Behave

What can you do about a toddler who just can't seem to behave? Parents are often aggravated when their children won't behave as desired in certain settings, such as houses of worship and restaurants. They expect a toddler to sit still, listen quietly, and engage in conversation only when she is addressed. Good luck!

The first question you should ask yourself is, "How old is my child again?" At this age, there is no way that she's going to act like an adult. Second, consider why your child would be enjoying any of these activities in the first place. There's nothing fun about being quiet, still, and mannerly. Expecting her to do this and to do it well is setting yourself up for a big disappointment. You are simply asking for much more than your toddler can provide.

This does not mean you should avoid going places that will require better behavior from your child. In fact, learning comes from doing, so going to these places is a perfect way for her to begin to learn acceptable behavior. Introducing her to these settings is a good idea because you cannot avoid taking her out forever. So take her with you, but also take along some things to keep her occupied—quiet activities, such as a book, crayons and paper, or a stuffed animal.

It is a good idea to plan to attend such places, but don't plan on staying very long. When your toddler starts getting fidgety and restless and you notice that she has lost interest in the activities you brought along, it's time to go! Staying will only result in her increasing frustration, which she will express *loudly*. You may only make it through the appetizers, but it's a good place to start.

Learning to Share

No one is going to argue that sharing is not a good thing. We are not born knowing how to share, however, and toddlers have a very difficult time with the concept. Some are afraid that if they share a toy, they might not get it back. Others feel the need to hold onto certain objects and simply cannot share them. To begin teaching the lesson of sharing, gently ask your child if it would be okay if his friend John played with his truck. If your toddler says, "No!" (as he probably will), don't push. If he does agree to share, don't let the other child keep the object for too long. Return the toy to your child so that your toddler realizes it is safe to share. Yelling and screaming that he is selfish or insisting that he share will backfire on you. As with all other things toddler, if he knows that not sharing will irritate you, he won't share.

> A good way to teach sharing is to share with your child. For example, if you have a cookie, offer to share it with him. Offer to share your chair with him if he will share his blanket with you. This will help him to see that sharing need not be unpleasant—and can even be fun!

As you are beginning to understand, a toddler's world is fraught with minefields of helplessness, confusion, excitement, and many other overwhelming feelings. Toddlers learn, grow, and change at an incredible rate, so what was normal for your toddler yesterday may be completely uncharacteristic for him today. If you can loosen up and be patient, you will find that there are more good days than difficult ones. A sense of humor won't hurt either!

Part Three

The Testy Threes (36–48 Months)

More Changes, More Challenges

No matter what is happening with your toddler today, you can be sure of one thing: it will be completely different tomorrow, in a few days, and in a few months! Although physical growth slows a bit during this period, your toddler's brain keeps expanding at an incredible pace. Her weight and height are increasing at about the same rate, and she remains ever fascinated by her little body. She may have spent her first 3 years figuring out how to get some control over her body, but now the real fun is beginning. She is discovering all of the things a body can *do*. When you think about it, you can see what an overwhelming job this can be for a tiny person. She has quite a job ahead of her!

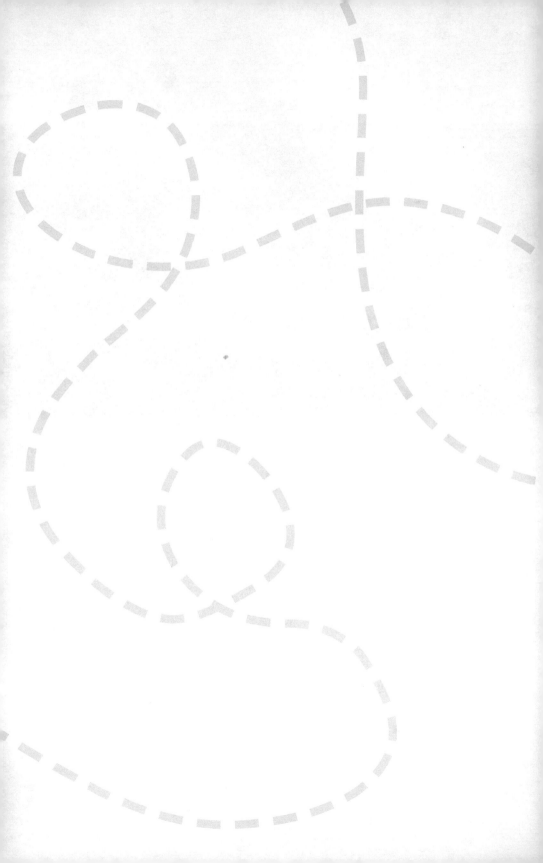

7

Physical Development

Sleep and Your Toddler—Finding the Best Fit

By now, your toddler is spending approximately half of her time in bed sleeping. Some toddlers still need an afternoon nap, whereas others will have abandoned a nap completely by this stage. Most toddlers do better if they can have a short rest in the afternoons, as this helps them make it through the remainder of the day. It also makes them a lot easier and a lot more fun to be around! Some parents complain that although their toddlers have been sleeping pretty well up to this point, all of a sudden they cannot fall asleep, and it isn't because of fear or distress. Remember that your child is growing and changing; perhaps she simply needs a different bedtime. If she does not seem tired at her normal bedtime, consider moving it to 15 to 30 minutes later. If she's getting a nap later in the afternoons, she is not going to be ready to go to bed early.

From Crib to Bed

During the 36- to 48-month stage, a toddler is typically ready to move from the crib to a bed. You're probably very excited because this symbolizes movement toward autonomy and your toddler reaching another milestone, but you also may be worried because she will be able to get out of bed whenever she wants, which means you may never have peace again!

When you are planning for your toddler to make the transition from crib to bed, it is best if you can include her and encourage her participation. Take her with you to pick out a new bed. If possible, let her choose between one or two beds and buy the one she wants. It might also be time to repaint her room and make other changes that are age-appropriate. Usually, a toddler will be excited about her new bed. Let her help decorate her room and pick some books and toys that she would like to have near her. This will give her room a "homey" feel, and she will have a sense of familiarity with it. You might also let

You may have to tweak your toddler's sleep schedule a bit in order to have it fit her needs during this time.

your child pick out some family photos or other pictures that she enjoys. Anything that can make her bedroom seem like a special, safe place is fine. If your toddler is truly spending a lot of time in her room, then it is necessary for it to be a place that she enjoys; this will also help limit any defiance over not going to bed.

Bedtime Rituals

Just as you did when she was younger, establish a ritual with the new bed and room as she is preparing for bed. Perhaps you can keep a stack of books next to your toddler's bed so that she can pick one for you to read to her at night. Maybe she'd prefer to sing along to a favorite song on a CD or tape player. Whatever she picks, make sure that it is an activity that will calm her but includes you as well. Try to stick to this ritual and be as consistent as you can about her bedtime. It may take a while for her to get used to the new arrangement, so try to stick with this routine for three to five nights to see if it will "take." If the routine doesn't appear to be working, abandon it and try something else.

Take Care with Timeouts

One other thing to watch out for is sending your toddler to her bedroom as punishment. If your toddler equates her bedroom or her bed with punishment or something else unpleasant, you are going to have a difficult time getting her to *want* to go to her room. Make sure you have another place in the house designated for timeouts, preferably a place that is not seen as fun, such as a quiet place or a specific chair.

Eating with the Family

Even though your toddler has gotten older and probably enjoys more foods than she used to, she is still going to have difficulties with eating. She will still tend to be messy and spill things—a lot. She may only eat peanut butter and bananas or some other particular food, while refusing anything else that is placed in front of her. Although you will be tempted to worry that your child is becoming malnourished, look at the bigger picture. Your toddler will eat when she is hungry, and eventually, bananas and peanut butter are going to become boring.

Trying New Foods

It's just a matter of time before she slowly starts testing other foods to see if she likes them. For the time being, if you wish to introduce new foods to her, go ahead; just don't expect too much. If you insist that she

Your toddler will eat when she is hungry, and eventually, bananas and peanut butter are going to become boring.

try sweet potatoes, for example, place a bite on her plate along with her other food. Do not make an issue of it and insist that she try it. Simply leave it there and see if her curiosity gets the better of her. If it doesn't, you haven't wasted a lot of food, and you can try another food at the next meal.

Family Meals

This stage is also a great time to incorporate family meals into your routine. Parents are extremely busy these days, and for many families, meals are eaten out, in front of the TV, or on the run. If possible, set aside at least one or two nights a week on which the family has dinner together. This is a great time for your toddler to interact with the rest of the family and to begin to observe others who have much better table manners!

But don't think you're going to start instilling wonderful manners in your toddler just yet. You'll be doing well to get your toddler to eat with a spoon and a fork. Instead, concentrate on making mealtime a pleasant experience that your toddler will look forward to. Manners, like developing a finer palate, will come later. Your toddler is old enough at this time to participate in the preparation of a meal. You can let her pull apart the lettuce for a salad or put ice in the glasses on the dinner table. She will enjoy it, taking pride in having accomplished something, and this will help make mealtime more pleasant. You are no doubt going to spend more time preparing the meal and cleaning up afterward if you do this, but it will be worth it for your child's development.

> Find some simple tasks that she can do all on her own or with some supervision from you and let her go.

Eating Out

Many parents say that they absolutely will not take their toddler to a restaurant. This is understandable because toddlers have a knack for showing their cranky, mischievous, and surly sides in public. However, if you don't start taking them to restaurants, when do you expect them to learn how to behave in public? You might first try taking your toddler to lunch at a restaurant before moving to dinner. Often, toddlers are less tired and more agreeable at this time of day. If you want to go out for dinner, go early. Toddlers don't do well when a reservation is for 8 PM. Instead, try going to a restaurant between 5 and 7 PM. Toddlers are a lot less grumpy at this hour, and they are usually hungry. If your toddler hasn't had her usual nap that day, don't expect her to be on her best behavior.

When going out to eat, be sure to pick a restaurant that is kid-friendly. In other words, make sure other children are around or the restaurant is one in which the other patrons should expect and won't mind having children present. Take along some quiet toys for your toddler to enjoy. After all, your toddler is not an adult! She is not going to sit like a little lady with her hands folded in her lap until it is time to go home. Plan to spend as little time at the restaurant as possible. Don't languish over a four-course meal. Your toddler may be able to handle an hour to an hour and a half, but after that, you're really asking for trouble. If you're not sure whether your toddler's going to eat anything on the menu, bring along some snacks. You can call ahead to find out if this is appropriate at that particular restaurant if you're not sure.

Whatever you do, don't avoid going out and enjoying time with your family simply because your toddler has to come along, too. The message here is really to plan ahead, maintain reasonable expectations, and go forth with a sense of humor and a heap of patience.

I Thought We Were Done with Toilet Training!

Perhaps you're one of those lucky parents whose toddler got the knack for toilet training down early, and you have never looked back. Accidents have been few and far between for your toddler, and for the most part, toilet training is no longer an issue. For the rest of you, understand first that you are in the majority. Toilet training is a process—it doesn't last a specific length of time. Your toddler is growing and changing, and so is his bladder. Until that bladder is fully developed, there are going to be problems. Urinating accidents are very normal for toddlers. Keep in mind that your toddler's world is getting bigger and bigger so his focus may not be on toilet training. He is more likely to want to concentrate on play and forget to go to the bathroom. He is undergoing many changes all at once and may not have the coping skills to handle everything that is happening to his body.

Fear

One reason toddlers seem to have more accidents at this age is a fear of toilets. A toddler is not afraid of the toilet that he has learned to use on a regular basis in his own home. However, as you are taking him to more new places and he is in more unpredictable circumstances, he will be faced with unfamiliar bathrooms and toilets. Many toddlers are uneasy and scared of toilets that they don't recognize. Don't laugh at or scold him; simply help him to understand that the new toilet is just like the one he has at home. If he is having accidents repeatedly in certain places, such as preschool, there might be a reason, and the situation should be checked out.

How to React to Accidents

The important thing to remember during this time is not to criticize or overreact. Although you may want to say, "I can't believe you wet your pants after all this time," don't do it. This will embarrass or humiliate him. Typically, toddlers are even more concerned about soiling accidents than you are. Remember that this is also something that they can use to test you. If you can manage to have a minor reaction, your toddler will likely have fewer accidents, resulting in less frustration for your toddler and for you.

Pull-up Pants and Diapers

Pull-up pants are popular these days, and they are great for those times when you worry that your toddler might have an accident. Because pull-ups resemble real underwear, make sure that you use them only occasionally. Letting him wear pull-ups during the day may actually send a message to the toddler that it's *okay* to have an accident in his pants. This is not the message you want to be sending, so use pull-ups sparingly. Use them when you know that time or circumstances may not allow your toddler to make it to the bathroom on time. A long car trip is an example of a time when pull-ups might be useful.

Parents often want to avoid letting their toddlers wear diapers at night even though "accidents" continue to occur. Parents may think that if they allow nighttime diaper wearing, they are somehow silently giving permission for their toddlers to have accidents. This is not true. If you know that your toddler cannot stay dry throughout the night, why put him or you through the agony of having to get up in the middle of the night, change sheets, change him, and put him back to bed? Your toddler will eventually want to stay dry and will have the ability to stay dry. Letting him wear diapers at night is not going to hurt him.

> **Because pull-ups resemble real underwear, make sure that you use them only occasionally. Letting him wear pull-ups during the day may send a message to the toddler that its *okay* to have an accident in his pants.**

Whatever you do, try not to worry too much. Your toddler is certainly not going to be wearing diapers when he goes to elementary school. He really will develop the ability to take care of himself, and he will get there in his own time!

More Sexual Exploration: What *Is* Normal?

Remember, this is the time that toddlers are learning about what their bodies can do, and what could be more fascinating than a part of the body that is "private?" Sexual exploration is normal. How much is normal? That seems to be the debatable question.

Different Conversations

If your toddler announces to you that he can make his penis big, you do not need to worry that he is quickly becoming a sexual deviant. He has merely learned that he can control some of his body, and he is proud of this accomplishment. Your best response to this sort of behavior is to say something like, "Yes, you certainly can, but that is best done in the privacy of your bedroom." Undoubtedly, he is going to ask you why. It will be up to you to give a short explanation that touching one's private parts is normal, but it is not to be done in public or shown off. This is a good time to continue the discussion about "good touches" and "bad touches."

Playing Doctor

The toddler who doesn't play some sort of "doctor" game is rare. Some will manage to play doctor with a friend, and you may never know it. Still others will get caught, and it will be up to you to handle the situation appropriately. Don't scream or jerk the children apart. Calmly say, "I notice you two are playing doctor. It's time for you to stop and do something else." Most kids will forget about it almost immediately. Later, remind your toddler about privacy and the things you have taught him about exploring his body.

Often, someone else (a teacher, for example) will catch your child playing doctor. Unfortunately, not everyone is prepared to deal with this, and it may be handled badly, with your toddler left feeling he is in trouble. He may also feel humiliated and embarrassed. He may get the message that his body is dirty or bad, and exploring it ought to be done in a secretive, sneaky way. If this happens, have a talk with your toddler and explain that his teacher was merely surprised and that what your toddler did was not bad. If a child senses overreaction, he is likely to repeat the behavior, feeling that there must be something dangerous and exciting about it if everyone is screaming "No!"

> **If you find your toddler and a friend playing "doctor," don't scream or jerk the children apart. Do your best not to make the issue into a big deal.**

When Your Toddler Is *Too* Interested

You should only begin to worry if your toddler appears to be overly interested in his genitals. Being too interested means that he is preoccupied to the point that he cannot seem to leave them alone. Consult your pediatrician to make sure that there's nothing wrong, such as a skin irritation or rash that he may simply be trying to scratch. If, on the other hand, there is some other problem, such as possible abuse or extreme anxiety, your pediatrician will know how to direct you to help correct the problem.

Toddlers are incredible human beings. Nothing is more joyful than having a happy, healthy toddler in your home. As you have seen, problems are going to occur, but they can also be overcome. You should enjoy the time you have with your toddler because it ends so quickly. Before you know it, your toddler will be packing for college, and you'll wonder why his tantrums, the food fights, and his other antics ever drove you so crazy.

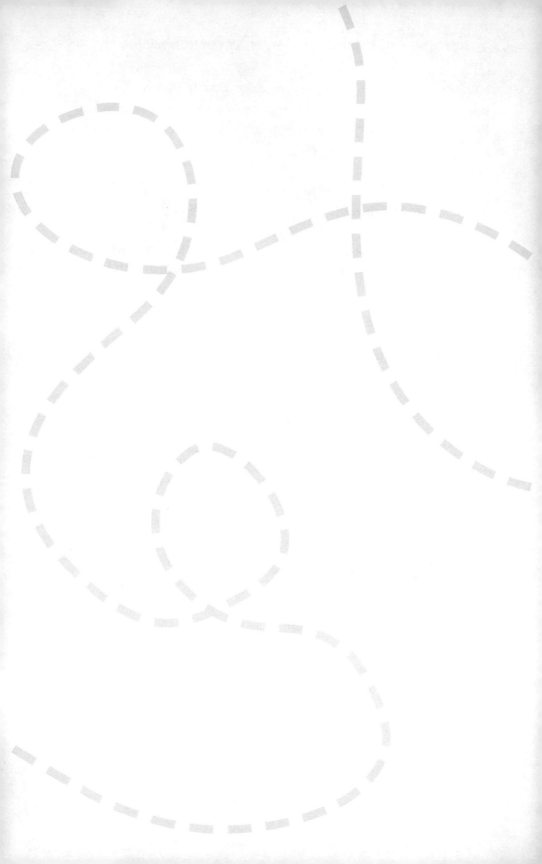

8

Cognitive Development

Fantasy and Imaginative Play

Toddlers really begin to show off their incredible imaginations between ages three and four. They can make almost anything come alive and will talk to almost anything as well. This is a great time to get your toddler involved in activities that allow her to use her creative abilities. Pretending is lots of fun, too, because a toddler can take on any role she wishes and become anyone that she wants to be.

Imaginary Friends

Don't be surprised if your toddler creates an imaginary friend. Your toddler might develop a friend that has a name, a personality, likes, dislikes, appetites, and fashion sense! Some parents are quick to brush off the imaginary friend as just that—imaginary—but you shouldn't do this because your child's friend is very important to her.

An imaginary friend provides opportunities for your child to develop her conversational abilities. The friend may also become her confidante with whom she shares secrets. Imaginary friends are very real to the toddler, and if you discount her friend, your toddler is likely to become hurt or angry. Fortunately, the world has not made a toddler skeptical yet, and this is a fun time for her.

If your toddler insists on "Libby" having a place at your dinner table, it is much easier to go along with your toddler than to resist. Libby may need something to eat, and you may have to prepare an extra plate. Only you can decide how far you want to go in including Libby in the family's life. It is best to let your toddler have her imaginary friend because soon she will turn to other activities and Libby will be gone.

The only time you should discourage your toddler's imaginary friend is if your toddler is using her friend to get out of trouble. For instance, if your toddler breaks something and suggests that Libby did it, you cannot let this slide. Rather, you'll need to explain to your toddler that she is responsible, not Libby, and that she is the one who will have consequences. If your toddler insists that she *and* Libby did something wrong, it's perfectly all right to go along with your toddler on this, but emphasize that there will be consequences for both of them.

Let's Pretend

Pretending can become quite elaborate during this time. Almost anything is food for the toddler's imagination. Most of us have played in the mud as children, and many of us have made mud pies. It's fun to have a toddler describe to you how she made the mud pie, what flavor it is, and how it ought to be eaten. Some toddlers like to use disguises or other "props" to dress and transform themselves into someone else. Others can change a stick into a mighty sword. Still others become mommies, daddies, circus animals, and so forth. "Let's pretend" is not only entertaining but educational as well.

Here are some great ways to introduce more imaginary play into your child's life:

- Make finger puppets out of old gloves or hand puppets from socks. Let your toddler draw on faces and fun details with a marker to create a character. Once done, your toddler can "talk" through or to her puppets.

- Ask your toddler to make up a story to tell you at bedtime.
- Write down characters or story titles on pieces of paper. Put the pieces of paper into a bowl and have your toddler pick one to act out.
- Buy or make costumes for dressing up. Party stores carry inexpensive hats, hairpieces, and other items that are great "pretend" starters.
- Gather some objects from around the house and have your toddler make up new uses for them.
- Have your toddler pretend she is a bird, a pig, a car—anything that moves. Ask her, "What would you say if you were a car?"

The list goes on and on, but you get the idea. Because a toddler will use just about anything to play with, you should use all the resources you can find!

> Play "Let's Pretend." For example, pretend you are at the doctor's office, a fancy party, a restaurant, or the beach. Let her pick the character she wishes to be and let her pick who you will be. The two of you can then act out a story involving those characters.

TV and Movie Influences

If your toddler watches television or movies, it is important to remember that these images can be either productive or destructive. For example, if your child watches a movie in which the main character is a hero who does good things, he may want to pretend that he is the same action hero. On the other hand, if your toddler sees a movie in which there is a bad guy who beats up other bad guys, he may want to pretend to be the bad guy who can beat up other bad guys. Although there is nothing inherently wrong with such play, you may want to suggest to your toddler that it's more fun to be the good guy. Whatever role he chooses to play, there is not much that can go wrong unless he hurts someone else—or himself.

Little Conversations

At this age, you will find that your toddler talks to anything and anyone—you, herself, her toys—and even no one or nothing at all. Toddlers learn speech by hearing and imitating, so unless a toddler can practice speech out loud, she has trouble internalizing it. It is not necessary to engage with your toddler when she is rambling on and on because many times she is just trying words out to see how they sound.

Ways to stir up conversation for your toddler might include: asking her to make up a story; using words that rhyme to make up a song together; or asking your toddler to "write" a letter to someone (of course, you'll have to write it, but she can tell you what to say!).

Teasing

Part of the problem with speech during this time is that toddlers learn to tease and to call names. Teasing is a difficult concept for a toddler to understand.

Some toddlers have very thick skins, and when they are teased, it rolls right off their backs. Others are quite sensitive and take everything to heart. If teasing occurs on a regular basis in your family, consider your child's temperament. There is nothing wrong with kidding around, but her feelings should be considered. Remember, toddlers learn how to behave by watching and modeling you. If your teasing tends to be a little on the harsh side, your toddler is apt to take this behavior and direct it toward other children.

If you have teased your toddler and she seems to have hurt feelings, help her to understand that nothing was meant by it, but also admit that your teasing was harsh and say that you're sorry. If you observe your toddler teasing others in a cruel way, pull her aside and ask her how she might feel if she were in her friend's shoes. If other children are teasing your toddler, resist the urge to step in and stop it. Wait and observe to see if your toddler's feelings are even affected. If they are not, you don't need to do anything. If you sense that your child is becoming frustrated and upset, then it is time to for you to step in and stop the conversation.

Name-calling

"Meanie, Dumbo, Stupid, Baby." You've certainly heard all of these and probably could come up with at least twenty more. Name-calling is not nice. If family members are calling your toddler names at home, then she is apt to call her friends names as well; this is not going to make her very popular among her friends. This is the perfect age to teach your child that other people have feelings that are important for your toddler to consider. Your toddler will not grasp this concept completely, but you need to repeat it to her anyway. Ask her how she would feel and what she would do if someone were to call her a bad name. Help her to understand that what she is doing is not kind and that her friends will not want to play with her if she calls them names.

Name-calling by other children toward your toddler should be handled in the same way as teasing. You are not going to be able to protect your toddler from being called names by other children, or from being teased, but there are valuable lessons to learn from both.

Stranger Danger

Between the ages of three and four, many toddlers become quite outgoing. Because they like to talk and have a need to talk, they will talk to anyone, including strangers. Unfortunately, our world today is not as safe as it once was, and talking to strangers can be dangerous. Now is the perfect time to teach children not to "talk to strangers." Along with this goes the lesson of not going anywhere with a stranger, even though your toddler may be told that you have approved it. There are many programs available to teach you how to keep your toddler safe and you'll do well to investigate them.

Although it is important to teach your toddlers caution, you don't want them to become completely avoidant when it comes to talking to others; after all, there is nothing wrong with a friendly "hello" or smile. Toddlers aren't very good judges of character at this age, however, and they can't differentiate between a healthy interaction with a stranger and a dangerous one. If you are going to err, it would be best to err on the side of caution and encourage your toddler not talk to anyone that she does not know.

Other experts suggest that rather than teaching your toddler to avoid strangers, you should tell your toddler that he is not to go anywhere with anyone unless he asks the adult who is with him. This makes a lot of sense because the toddler can "transfer" the authority to other caretakers—the babysitter, schoolteacher, grandparent, or whoever is caring for her. Whoever is looking after your child at the moment can be the one he must ask, and this will ensure his safety.

More Fears and New Phobias

Now that your toddler is getting a little older, you'd think that the fears and phobias she experienced earlier would have gone away. This may be true, but unfortunately, they may simply have been replaced by others. During this time, toddlers are generally afraid of going away from home. Because home is where they have spent the vast majority of their time and it is the place in which they feel the safest, going to other locations, even someplace as familiar as a grandparent's home, can bring on anxiety. Trying to reason with your child by saying something like, "You've been to Grandma's before so there's nothing to be scared of," is not going to work. Understand that new situations and change can be hard for a toddler, and the most common reaction is one of anxiety and fear.

"What If…?"

Don't be surprised if your toddler starts asking, "What if you get a divorce?" or "What if you die?" This can happen particularly if the toddler has observed or been involved these stressful circumstances. She will take these events and personalize them and wonder what is going to happen to her.

The best thing you can do with fears and phobias at this age is to reassure her, reassure her, and reassure her some more. Don't label your toddler's fears as silly, and don't criticize her. Help her understand that fears are normal but in fact she is going to be all right. Providing her with a sense of stability and security is the best gift you can give her during this time.

Just about anything can be something to fear for a toddler this age. A child may be frightened about becoming hurt or worried that things are going to break. This is when the "what ifs" really come into play. Toddlers have just enough knowledge now to be scared. In other words, the more your toddler knows, the more questions she will have and the more fears she can potentially develop.

Look What I Can Do! Development of Independence

With the acquisition of more information, more speech, and more experiences, your toddler is going to strive for even more independence then she did during the trying twos. Independence is important, but it can be very hard to achieve, and it is up to you to make this accomplishment possible by creating opportunities for your toddler to exercise her independence.

Learning to Make Choices

As toddlers, we didn't have difficult decisions to make, as we do now, but we did use our limited decision-making experience to develop the ability to make good choices. For the same reason, our own toddlers need the opportunity to make basic decisions and choices for themselves. The easiest way to help a toddler achieve independence is to offer choices. For example, you can offer two choices for dinner and let your child pick. Or, if your toddler has several books that she really likes, let her choose which book she would like you to read to her before she goes to bed. Some parents cringe about this next one, but it really is okay to let your toddler pick her outfit for the next day. It may not match, or it may not be what you would have picked, but she is not going to hurt anyone by choosing the "wrong" colors!

> We all have to make decisions on a daily basis, but where did we learn to make the choices that we do? For most of us, it started early when we were toddlers ourselves.

As much you can, encourage your toddler to do things herself. Buttoning her sweater, brushing her teeth, and washing her hands are all things she needs to learn to do on her own. She may not do a perfect job, but she is not going to suffer from making these types of choices and they are important aspects of her development.

Here are some simple choices that you can let your toddler make. You'll notice all of them involve two items, not more. Having to choose at all can be overwhelming enough for a toddler without adding more choices!

- Pick between two items of similar clothing (for example, the red shirt or the blue one).
- Select a book to read from two choices.
- Choose between two foods (carrots or peas, not broccoli or ice cream).
- Pick from two TV programs.
- Choose whether to take a bath before or after dinner.
- Choose whether to play outside or in her room.

Whatever you do, try not to get into a battle of wills during this time. If your toddler is insistent that she doesn't want to read a story together but would rather sing a song with you, just do it. It you're trying to instill some resilience and self-sufficiency in your child, this can be very trying a good bit of the time; however, with each new level of independence comes a boost in self-confidence, and your toddler will thrive because of it.

Emotional Changes

9

Making Friends

Part of the joy of watching your toddler grow up is watching her develop relationships with other children. These relationships will enrich her life in so many ways, and she will develop her first set of social skills as a result. One of the best ways to start introducing other children into your toddler's life is to join a play group or other organized group activity. Many children go to "Mother's Day Out" programs. About once or twice a week, toddlers go and spend the good part of the day with each other playing games, doing crafts, and running about in the playground. Such programs are a perfect opportunity for you to give yourself a little free time while providing your child with some healthy peer experiences.

This is also a great time to invite one of your children's friends over to play. Some parents exchange babysitting duties this way; one parent will send her children over to a friend's home so that she can have a free afternoon. The next week, the play date is held at another child's home. Sometimes it is less overwhelming for a toddler to just have one child around than to be in a group. Either option is appropriate.

Arguments

What do you do if your child has a friend that she seems to argue with a lot? First, don't be quick to dismiss the friend. Toddlers are notorious for saying things to one another with little regard for how feelings might be affected. Second, don't rush in to scold your child and take up for the other child. Instead, comfort the child if necessary and try to divert both children's attention to something else. Remember, at this age, toddlers believe that the world revolves around them. Although you should begin to teach your toddler empathy now, it will not come naturally to her.

Biting and Hitting

What if your child's friend is constantly biting or hitting your child? Your first tendency would normally be to not have that friend over again. But this is not always necessary. If you can, try to separate the two children while explaining to them that hitting, biting, and any other activity that hurts another person is not going to be tolerated. If the behavior continues, you might want to speak to the child's mother. If none of this works, and this particular child continues to be aggressive, it might be time to find your toddler another playmate.

The Parent as Diplomat

So how do you deal with other toddlers' parents? We would all like to think that "our little angel" could never have done whatever it is he's being accused of doing; however, we also know that, at times, our own toddler is likely to be guilty. Approach other parents with caution if you plan to discuss their children's behavior. Understandably, parents are often quite defensive about their children and don't take negative comments about them well. If possible, wait until you see a pattern of behavior that is disturbing rather than an isolated incident before approaching the other parent. Find a way to say what you want without blaming or criticizing. Rather than saying, "Tommy just won't stop hitting my child, and somebody needs to do something about his temper," try being a bit more gentle. For example, say, "Tommy seems a little more aggressive than usual. Is everything okay with him?" This conveys a tone of concern rather than one of irritation or blame. You'll get much further with other parents if you deal with them in this manner.

Getting Your Toddler Involved with Others

Whatever you do, do not let your toddler become isolated. Parents are so busy with work, outside obligations, and other family matters that they may forget that a toddler's social life is just as important as their own. This is the first opportunity for your toddler to learn sharing, social skills, and the wonderful benefits of friendships, and it is extremely important that he have these experiences before he reaches school age.

There are plenty of activities that your toddler and a friend or several friends can participate in with your supervision. How about making your own sundae (or pizza, or cookie)? Put all of the ingredients for a sundae on a table that has been covered with a paper tablecloth. Scoop the ice cream in the cups and then let the children decorate their sundaes as they prefer. Don't worry that they have too much or too little on their sundaes. This is about imagination and having fun. For a pizza, cook small individual-sized cheese pizzas or cut up a large pizza and then put out toppings for the toddlers to

Some parents wonder if this is a good time to start having sleepovers. The general rule is that toddlers are still too young for sleepovers. However, if there is a child with whom your toddler is particularly close and with whom he spends a lot of time, the two of them might do just fine having a sleepover together. For the most part, though it's usually best to wait until everyone is a little older.

pick. With cookies, set out icings, sprinkles, and other adornments so that they can decorate their own cookies.

There are a number of easy crafts that are fun for toddlers to personalize. Either buy or make inexpensive paper hats; then provide the kids with crayons, markers, and other decorations to add on. Inexpensive white T-shirts are also a good option for decorating fun. Gather together three or four rubber stamps and stamp pads or paint and let the children decorate their T-shirts. Everyone gets to take a T-shirt home, and it will be a fun reminder of the time they spent together.

Games are a great way to encourage interaction and the development of social skills. Make sure the toddlers are not playing a competitive game where someone "outdoes" the other. Toddlers are more interested in having fun and being silly. Some of the best games to play at this age are:

- Hot Potato
- Duck Duck Goose
- Tag
- Hide and Seek
- Simon Says

New Separation Issues

Because your toddler has likely developed some new fears, she may now have new and different concerns surrounding separation. For example, if she is afraid of being hurt, she may fear playing certain games or going to certain events that require physical activity. If she is afraid of something happening to you, she may not want to let you out of her sight. She may be anxious about visiting a friend whose family is going through a lot of stress. Toddlers pick up on the stress of others and seem to have a great knack for knowing when something is wrong. If your toddler senses that a situation is different from the way it is ordinarily, she may not want to be a part of it.

New Situations

Some toddlers make the transition to group activities and day care without ever looking back. They are happy to be in the new environment and can't wait to play with the other children. But just as quickly as your toddler may have become accustomed to this situation, she can rapidly decide that it is no longer where she wants to be. Something may have happened at this particular place that was unpleasant, or she may not want to be there for some other reason. Whatever the issue, you need to find out what it is and address it. If your child has new anxieties about separating from you, respect this. It may be that she has recently spent a lot more time with you and does not wish to be away from you just yet. On the other hand, she may have a genuine fear of something but have a difficult time expressing it. Your best bet is to push her—but not too hard!

Pushing your toddler—just a little bit—when she's afraid is a good way to see if her anxieties are real and serious problems or just minor anxieties. Sometimes, a toddler will voice fear, but when she is encouraged just a little bit, she will go ahead and move along.

When your toddler's fears are very real and very large, resistance is the only way she knows to deal with them. If your child is increasingly resistant about an activity, person, or place, try to determine what the problem is and whether it is something that can be corrected. Sometimes the very best answer is to go along with your toddler and not back her into a corner. As with all things toddler, forcing the issue will not work to your benefit.

Helping Your Toddler Deal with Fear

If your toddler's fears are unfounded, find a way to prove that to her. The best way to do this is to provide evidence that what she thinks is not true. For example, if your toddler is scared to go to day care because she doesn't want to be away from you and thinks something might happen to you, try taking her to the day care for just a little while. Have her stay for a few minutes, and then when you return, she will begin to understand that nothing has happened to you and you really *do* come back. Increase the amount of time you spend away from her and this fear will decrease. If your toddler is positively convinced that there is something hiding in her closet, turn on the light in the closet before she goes to bed. Rummage through the closet and when you "discover" that no one is hiding in there, exclaim excitedly, "Look, no one's there!" Try to resist talking rationally about your child's fear because she will only hear that you think she's being silly. Some amount of fear is healthy and normal and should not be discouraged. What you're trying to do is help your toddler face her fears, find evidence that her fears are unfounded, and move forward.

Manipulative Crying: What Should You Do?

You may be applauding and complimenting your child by telling her that she has become such a big girl; however, you've also likely noticed that she still cries—a lot. This is normal, and the reasons are varied. Some toddlers don't have enough language skills to enable them to express their emotions adequately. When they become overwhelmed with a particular feeling, crying is a natural response. Other toddlers are simply very sensitive. This is the toddler who falls apart with the least bit of provocation and for what seems like no reason. Everything is a huge deal, and there is a tendency to overreact. Still other toddlers cry frequently because they have gotten positive reinforcement for it. Often parents are protective and reactive, and when their toddlers cry they are quick to rush in to give the toddler relief. Doing this too much and too often results in a child who knows that when she cries, somebody will come running.

Be Observant

Whatever the reason is for the crying, there are ways to temper it and lessen its frequency. First, be observant. Is your toddler crying regularly at a particular time of day? She may be tired, hungry, or bored. She cannot soothe herself so she cries with the hope that someone else will take care of her. Does your toddler tend to cry around certain people? If so, she may be uncomfortable around these individuals, or they may be doing something that inadvertently causes her to cry. Does she cry only when she knows you are watching? Then she might be crying because she knows that it will get your attention and evoke your sympathy. By watching your toddler closely and not being overly critical, you can find out the real reasons for your toddler's cries. She may have a very legitimate reason for crying and really need you to intervene.

Encourage Your Toddler's Independence

Second, encourage her independence. Doing so not only enhances her self-esteem, it also builds her confidence. Many toddlers do not want to take new risks and cry out of fear. When you encourage your child to try new things, you are in effect telling her, "You can do this, and I won't let you get hurt." When she sees that what she has been avoiding no longer needs to be feared, the crying will begin to subside.

Excessive Crying or Whining

When crying or whining is excessive, one of the best things you can do is ignore it. Try to provide a distraction for your toddler, but do not give your full attention to the crying. If your toddler is seeking your attention and she is not getting it, she may increase her crying temporarily to see if "adding more heat" will get to you. There is nothing wrong with telling your toddler, "You are welcome to cry because you are frustrated and angry. I'm going to let you sit here by yourself and cry, and when you're finished, we can go for a walk." By doing this, you are acknowledging that her frustrations are real but also teaching that she is going to have to get herself under control without your babying her.

> When she sees that you are no longer going to jump every time she cries, she will likely resort to other ways of getting attention that are more healthy and pleasant.

Do not assume that all crying is manipulative and fake. Your child may have some very legitimate reasons for crying, and these cannot be ignored. Watching her carefully and seeking answers for her crying are crucial.

Part Four

More Things You Need to Know

The More You Know...

We've reviewed the basics about toddlers with regard to physical, cognitive, and emotional development. If that's not enough to make your head spin, there's even more that you need to know! Raising children takes much more than money and time if you want to do it right. Your toddler faces many new challenges and experiences. Is there a sibling to follow? Are there developmental issues that need to be addressed? Your toddler will need to learn socialization skills so that she can begin to develop relationships with her peers and others. You may be preparing her for preschool, or you may wonder if she is even ready to take this big step. You will probably be traveling more with your toddler, but what's the best way to do it without feeling overwhelmed? Learning good parenting strategies as well as ways to take care of yourself will help you through this trying time. If you feel that your education in toddlerhood may never end, you are right! But the more you know, the better off you *and* your toddler will be.

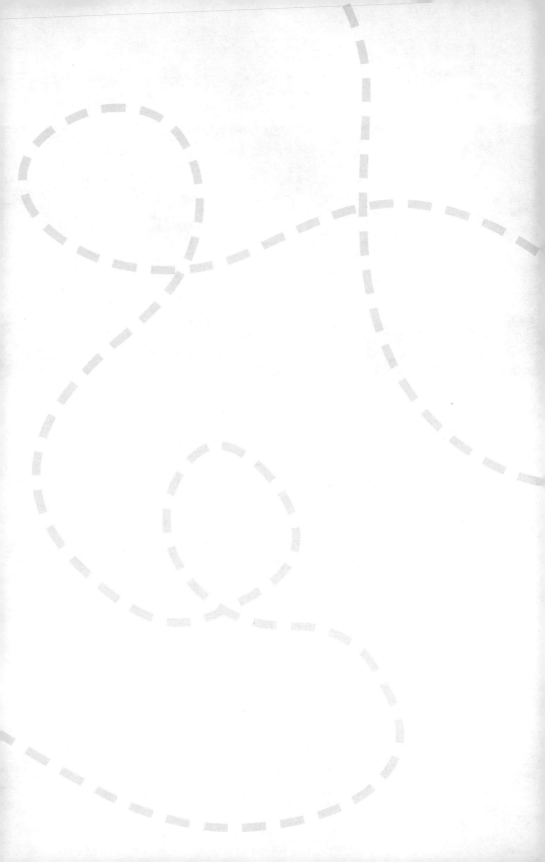

Adding Siblings to the Nest

10

How Far Apart in Age Should Siblings Be?

You've probably heard some version of this: you want to have a baby, but you want to make sure it's the *perfect* time to do so. So just when is the perfect time? Answer: if you wait until it's the perfect time, you'll never have a baby!

The same is true for adding siblings to your family. If you wait until your toddler is older; if you wait until he is over his tantrum stage; if you wait until he is potty trained; your child may never have brothers or sisters! The "if you waits" can be endless, and there is no right answer.

There is no scientific proof that toddlers born only a couple years apart have closer relationships with each other, although this is the reason many give when asked why they chose to have another baby very soon after their first. Likewise, there's no proof that spacing them further apart is best. You may want children close in age so you can get the diapers, sleepless nights, and other troubling times behind you more quickly. Other families may want a "rest" between children in order to recuperate.

What's Right for Mom?

Will the timing of your pregnancies make your children closer? Indeed not. We don't get to pick who is in our family, right? And that means there are some relatives that we just don't like! The same will be true for siblings. Some may be crazy about each other whereas others may not like each other as much. The timing has nothing to do with it—this one is a toss-up. Although there may be things you can do to improve the relationship between siblings, they will ultimately decide for themselves how close they want to be. Some experts suggest moms give themselves at least 18 months between pregnancies. This gives a mother's body time to readjust and prepare itself for another pregnancy. Others argue that a two- to three-year gap is better. This gives a child time with his parents before another child begins to demand attention. None of these times may sound right to you, and that is okay.

> Will the timing of your pregnancies make your children closer? No. Although there may be things your can do to improve the relationship between siblings, they will ultimately decide for themselves how close they want to be.

What's Right for the Family?

Rather than trying to pick the perfect time for a pregnancy based completely on age and your toddler's needs, you need to consider what works for you, too. How old are you? Was there a pregnancy complication that you may have to face the next time around? How are things in your career? Is this a good time to contemplate being away from work? Does your first child have any special needs or illnesses that have taken up most of your time and emotional resources? And speaking of emotional resources, are you ready to have another child clamoring for your attention?

Answer the questions that pertain to your family's situation honestly and without reservation. Are you ready to add another person to your clan given all the complications and challenges inherent in doing so? If the answer is no, listen to your heart and mind. Don't let others sway you or try to convince you that you are "doing it wrong." What works for one does not always work for another; this is a choice to be made within your immediate family (that means you and your spouse).

Only Children

When you are considering when the perfect time to have your next child might be, you may decide that you don't want any more children at all. Some parents feel guilty about making this choice. Is an only child destined to be a brat—spoiled and doted upon? Will she be lonely? Is she unfairly being denied the gift of a sibling? Just like the question of timing, there is no magic answer.

The stereotypical only child is lonely, spoiled, selfish, and somehow emotionally stunted, but this is *only* a stereotype. If your only child is any of these things, you have had some responsibility in that. Research shows that only children are just as happy, and often even happier, than children with siblings. They tend to be more academically and occupationally successful, as well as emotionally *more* healthy. Only children have been found to be more independent, adventurous, and often more popular with more age groups.

Whatever your decision is about whether to add children to your nest, the important thing is that you do what feels right to *you*. This cannot be stressed enough. Don't compare yourself to other families or cave in to pressure you feel from your extended family or friends. Take the time to consider all the pros and cons of having another child as well as your own feelings about whether adding another is healthy for you. If you do this, your answer will be as right as it can be!

Preparing Your Toddler for a New Arrival

If you have decided to add another child to your family, take a deep breath. Yes, it will be hard, there's no doubt about that. But who cares? No one ever said parenthood was an easy job! Whatever trepidation you may be feeling, remember your toddler will be even more anxious about the changes that will occur once a sibling comes along.

No Longer the Center of the Universe

First, consider the fact that until now, your toddler has been the center of your world and he knows it. In having another child, you are basically asking him to give up his throne to his successor! That is a very difficult thing for a toddler to handle. Forget trying to convince him that having a new baby is going to be fun and exciting. You would do better to assume that there will be jealousy and insecure feelings. Your toddler will probably feel that he is being overlooked, forgotten, and pushed aside. That is not going to engender warm, happy feelings about the new arrival.

> **The best thing you can offer a toddler before a new baby comes along is good coping skills. Make sure he already feels secure and happy in his existing family. Encourage his independence because this will give him a feeling of adequacy and will help him believe that he is *needed* by the new baby.**

From a toddler's point of view, it's bad enough that you left home and came back in a few days later with a new baby. Can you imagine what that would be like if you couldn't verbalize your feelings of jealousy and anxiety yet? If your child will be between 18 and 24 months old when Junior arrives, this *is* going to happen, and you will be restricted in what you can do to help him cope. You may find that your toddler regresses and begins acting as he did at an earlier age. He may try to strike the new baby in an attempt to say, "You don't belong here. It's time for you to go!" He may ignore the new baby altogether, somehow hoping the baby will magically disappear.

You'll have a little better luck with a toddler who is older and can understand generally what you are saying when you announce that he will be getting a new sister or brother. As your pregnancy progresses, so will your toddler's vocabulary and ability to understand what is happening.

Talking to Your Toddler About Your Pregnancy

Kids don't have a very good sense of time, so there is no reason to start discussing the pregnancy with your toddler from the very start. Experts advise that you wait until you are six months or more along for several reasons. If something happens and your pregnancy is ended, it's a difficult thing to explain to a toddler, and it's something that you'd rather not have to do. Also, if you tell your toddler too early, he may experience an increase in jealousy, anxiety, and other negative emotions that he just doesn't need to deal with. Ask friends and family to respect your request to wait to give this good news.

Preparing for a New Baby

Prepare, prepare, prepare. This should be your mantra during this time. Spend the time you have before your second baby is born helping the first one to get ready for the big invasion! Get her involved in play groups, a Mother's Day Out Program, or other activities if you haven't already done so. Having new places to go and new friends will help her establish her own life. There are also toddler classes designed specifically to help children prepare for the arrival of a sibling. Check to see if these are offered where you live because this is one of the best support systems you can have during this time.

If your toddler is still in a crib, and you are going to need that crib, get her out several months beforehand. You don't want to "take away" her bed right before the baby is due because your toddler is bound to feel pushed out. Take her with you to buy new sheets, bedding, and other things the new baby and she will need.

If there is to be a new person in the home, such as a babysitter or nurse, try to incorporate that person into your household *before* your baby is born. Too many changes are overwhelming for a toddler. This will give her a chance to get used to having a stranger in the house before the second stranger arrives.

As your due date approaches, let your toddler feel the baby kick. This gives her some idea that there is a *real* person in there. Ask her for help in picking out names, toys, and clothes for the baby. All of this will help increase your toddler's tolerance for the new baby who will be interfering with her life.

Handling Your Toddler when the Day Arrives

Whatever is going on, take a moment to stop, pay attention to your little one, and say goodbye. Do this even if it's the middle of the night so your toddler won't awaken the next morning to find that his whole world has been turned upside down and you are gone, too!

There are varying opinions on whether you should let your toddler come to the hospital. First, consider your toddler's age. The younger he is, the less important it is to have him visit. If you have an IV, stitches, or anything else that may cause your toddler distress when he sees it, you may want to skip the visit. Others say it is important to include your toddler in hospital visits so that he feels he is a part of the bigger picture. Whatever you decide to do, consider *not* making any promises ahead of time. This will give you the ability to assess your situation as it happens, and decide whether it is going to be beneficial for your toddler to visit.

Involving Your Toddler in the "New" Family

So the new baby has arrived at last, and you are ready to take her home. But what do you do about the toddler you have at home? Your toddler may be thrilled about, indifferent to, or full of dread about the prospect of having a sibling. But there is one thing he will want more than anything else—you! You have been gone, and he has missed you. It makes sense then that he will probably be pretty demanding about asking for your attention the minute you walk through that door.

> Some toddlers want to do everything the baby gets to do, such as bathing in the sink and being held and rocked. It's okay to indulge some of this because your toddler will get tired of it soon enough. Help your toddler focus on what he is "old enough" to do, and this will hurry the process along.

If you can, let your spouse or another adult hold the baby while you first make contact with your toddler. Tell him how much you missed him and ask him what he's been doing. Give lots of hugs and kisses and remind him that he is loved. Then it's time to introduce him to the baby. Ask nonchalantly if he'd like to see his new brother or sister. Don't make a big deal about it; stay as low-key as possible so that he doesn't feel threatened.

Jealousy and the New Baby

Your toddler will likely be jealous of the time you must spend with the baby. You should encourage his presence, if appropriate, but it's also okay to acknowledge to him that he is not getting what he wants at that minute because you are busy doing something else. Make it clear that when you are done taking care of the baby, you will play with him, read him a story, or deal with whatever issue he has raised. If you breastfed your toddler when he was a baby, he is likely to understand what you are doing when you breastfeed your infant. If not, you may have to find a way to explain it at an age-appropriate level. Don't be surprised if your toddler demands to be breastfed! After all, his new sister is getting to do it, so why can't he? Explain that he is a big boy and doesn't need to be breastfed anymore. Tell him that breast milk is for little babies only.

Helping with the New Baby

Is it appropriate to ask your toddler to do certain things for the baby? It depends. Some toddlers have a need to be useful and like doing things to be helpful. Others show no interest at all. Take your toddler's lead. If he wants to throw away the dirty diaper, there's no harm in letting him. If he wants to help bathe the baby, let him hand you the soap or wash the baby's back gently. Ask him to perform tasks that are age-appropriate and things that he can be successful doing. But do not let your toddler's sense of success come only from helping you with the baby. Encourage other experiences so that he does not begin to feel overly obligated toward his new sibling.

Handling Jealousy and Sibling Rivalry

Be prepared (there's that word again!) for your toddler to say about the baby, "I hate her." Remember, even though he may be fascinated and generally welcoming to his new sibling, he is still getting used to the idea that she is here to stay. Don't respond by saying something like, "You shouldn't say that. Stop being mean." If you give too much attention to it, he'll keep saying it because negative attention is better than no attention or the attention you are paying to his sibling. Second, if you scold him harshly about this, he is likely to feel guilty. If you think about it, he really has nothing to feel guilty about. He is a toddler, after all, and his whole world is being changed to accommodate someone else. There are times he probably really does dislike this little person. Handle the situation with respect and empathy for his feelings. Tell him that you understand why he might feel that way because he has been used to having Mommy and Daddy all to himself. Then try to talk about things he likes about his sibling.

If your toddler persists with this behavior, evaluate whether you are spending enough one-on-one time with him. Arrange to do something special, just the two of you. Talk to him about how neat it is to be the oldest. He gets to eat big-people food and play outside. He gets to play with all sorts of things that the baby can't. Whatever you can do to make your toddler feel special in his own right will be helpful.

Stepsiblings

We have talked about the new baby and its introduction into your toddler's life. But what about a stepchild? These days this is just as likely a scenario. It would be very normal for your toddler to have many of the same feelings about a stepbrother or stepsister as he might have about a new baby. Either way, whether it is a baby or a step-sibling, he is going to feel usurped and threatened. The techniques you use for introducing a stepsibling to the family should be similar to those used to introduce a new baby. Although you can't *make* your child accept these new family members, you should also explain to him that he must be kind and that you will treat everyone fairly. Above all, keep reminding him that he is loved no matter what or who may interrupt his life.

When Sibling Rivalry Becomes Physical

All toddlers fight at one point or another. Unless your toddler has a new stepsibling that is his age, you are going to have to watch out; you don't want your toddler hurting a new baby. Toddlers don't have a sense of their own strength and rarely *want* to hurt someone seriously. If you discipline by spanking, your toddler may even think his hitting is acceptable. In fact, studies show that children who are spanked tend to be more aggressive. If your toddler is beginning to hit, you will need to do several things. First, stop the behavior and explain that hitting is *not* okay. Separate the kids if you can. Second, tell your child that although it is normal for siblings to fuss—much like Mommy and Daddy, for example—there are better ways to resolve a dispute. Help him find age-appropriate methods to do so. For example, teach him to speak up rather than hit. Or talk with him about different ways he can handle an argument. Play out a scene with him to let him pretend he is resolving a problem.

Don't try to make your toddler feel guilty by saying something like, "I can't believe you'd do such a horrible thing to your sister." This sends the message that your toddler's feelings are wrong or that he is bad, not the behavior. Find a way to validate your toddler's feelings while expressing your disapproval about his behavior. You might say, "What you did hurt your sister. Can you remember how you felt when that happened to you?" Or "How might you feel if someone did that to you? Do you think that's how your sister felt?"

Set age-appropriate rules and make sure each child understands them. Let them know what the consequences will be if the rules are broken.

Instead of insisting to your toddler that he should love his sister, try showing him how the baby feels about him! If the baby looks at your toddler and smiles, tell him, "Look, she likes you!" If your toddler can make the baby giggle, praise him on how he is the only one who can do that! If your toddler realizes that the baby likes him and depends on him, he will feel needed, and he will find himself *wanting* to be involved with the baby.

Then stick to what you've told them. If the rules are broken, don't cave in; be consistent, and enforce your rules. When you observe your toddler engaging in "good" sibling behavior—for example, sharing, hugging, or playing well—tell him. Praise him for the good things he does and he will be more likely to do them again.

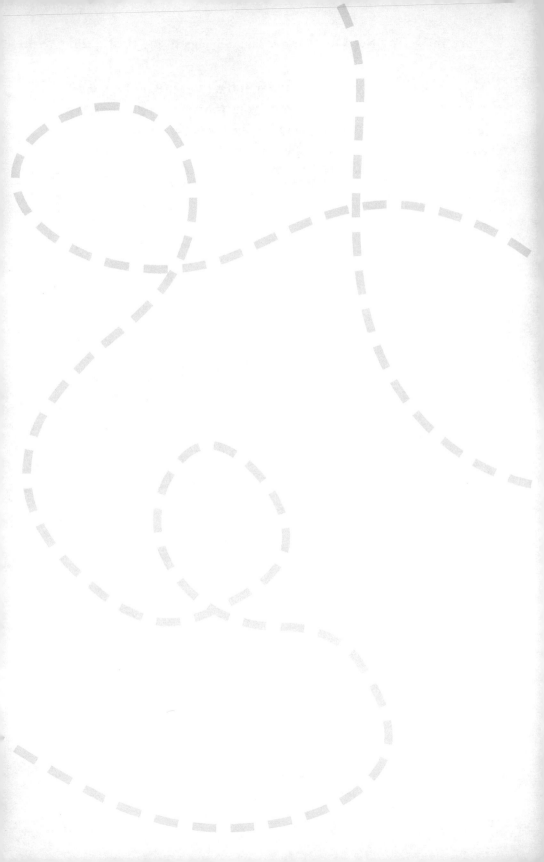

Developmental Issues

11

Speech and Language

All parents worry if their children don't acquire language at the same rate as their toddler's peers or siblings. Some chronological milestones have been set forth as the timeline in which speech is learned, but not every toddler will follow it. Your toddler's speech develops best if he is around others who are talking. In other words, the more exposure he has to hearing speech, the sooner he will be ready to talk. In some cases, however, toddlers will just refuse to talk or can't talk.

When should you worry?

If your child is not talking by the age of two, you may want to have his hearing checked. If he is deaf, he will not be able to mimic language. If his hearing is found to be fine, then wait a few months to see if he starts talking. Some children with slow language acquisition finally talk by the age of three. Other physical reasons for not developing language may be a neurological issue or autism.

By the age of three, most children are talking, but each toddler follows his own developmental path. There are a number of factors that can affect your child's speech development. In general, boys develop speech at a slower rate than girls. If you have a boy, don't compare him with any of the girls he may know. A child who has a twin or older siblings who talk a lot may find that he doesn't have a lot of reason to talk on his own. He always has someone else who can do his talking for him. So why bother learning? Also, if you are rushing in to do something for your toddler as the result of his gestures, he may be slower to talk. What's the point of learning if Mommy and Daddy are willing to do everything for me?

In addition, as you have read and experienced, toddlers have a finite amount of concentration and attention. If they are fully engrossed in learning other things, language may not be on their radar. When your child perfects whatever it is he is working on at the time, he can then give more of his attention to talking. Today many families are bilingual or have a caregiver who speaks little or no English. A child who is in this environment doesn't have as many opportunities for learning English. If speaking two languages is absolutely necessary in your home, you should realize that your toddler has to learn two different ways of talking so he may take longer to acquire speech.

Aphasia

If there are no physical reasons for the failure to acquire speech, the cause may be childhood aphasia, which means that a toddler has failed to meet normal speech and language developmental milestones. Basically, a child with aphasia does not develop speech in the order that is expected: words, phrases, and then sentences. Aphasia takes many forms. Some children understand words but cannot speak. Others can speak but have a poor understanding of what they are saying. Still others may know words but cannot master the rules of speaking, such as sentence construction and grammar. If you have concerns about your toddler's speech acquisition, watch for how he responds to you when you talk. Does he answer questions? Can he follow simple rules and instructions? Is he a "pointer," preferring to let you do the work so that he doesn't have to talk? If he appears to understand what he is gesturing toward, his problem is not aphasia. He is merely a little slower to acquire speech.

Seeking Help

If you remain worried that your child has not met normal developmental speech milestones, seek help from your pediatrician or a speech therapist. Some professionals may be quick to try to make you feel better and may discount your concerns in an attempt to alleviate your fears. If this is happening but you feel that your fears are reasonable, keep pushing until you get the help and answers you need.

Physical Coordination

The development of physical coordination is slow and unpredictable at best. One minute, your toddler is walking, and the next minute, he refuses to walk or appears unable to do so. Part of this is because until about the age of three, he will still demand that you pick him up and carry him with you if you are showing signs of walking away.

Another problem with physical coordination is that it requires a good bit of confidence. A toddler who does not feel *psychologically* safe with physical activity may resist development at an age-appropriate level. Maybe your toddler fell the last time she tried to run. Maybe she experiences frustration when trying to grip a pencil so she refuses to draw.

Developing Physical Skills

As with language, toddlers learn physical skills by observing and imitating what they see. If you think your child is behind in the development of her skills, try working with her to help her develop these skills before you really begin to worry. If walking is the problem, practice walking with her. Hold her hand and help her walk. Make the walk interesting so that she wants to be involved. Take her to a playground or another place where there is stimulating activity.

If she has trouble grasping small objects, find some things that are interesting to her and play "let's grab it." Put an item just out of her reach and cheer her on. Many problems with physical coordination have to do with a lack of interest or opportunity. Interest can be stimulated by opportunity, but mainly the motivation must come from within your toddler. Some children have more curiosity than others. On the other hand, opportunity is something you can readily offer.

If you think about it, learning to use your body is a very complicated process. There are so many things to master: crawling, walking, running, gripping small and large objects, drawing, writing, and so on. And while your toddler is learning all of this, she is supposed to be learning to communicate, too! Physical coordination may come along slowly, and its acquisition is highly individualized.

If your toddler is interested and has plenty of opportunities to develop her physical skills and still substantially lags behind, then it is time to consider whether there is a physical problem. A developmental specialist or your pediatrician can take a look at your toddler and determine whether she has gross motor delay. If she does, there are treatments specifically designed to help her attain these skills.

Vision

Toddlers usually don't know something is wrong with their vision because they don't have anything different to compare it to. Therefore, they rarely complain or are able to explain the nature of their difficulties. According to most pediatricians, you should be on the lookout for the following problems:

- Eyes that look crossed or don't move together; pupils that are different from one another in size
- Frequent headaches, dizziness, or nausea after doing activities that require "close-up" vision
- Bulging eyes
- Frequent squinting (not attributable to bright light) when looking at something
- Tilting of the head when looking at something
- Excessive swelling, tearing, redness, or crusting of the eyes
- Frequent sties or infections in which discharge from the eye is yellowish or greenish yellow
- Frequent clumsiness that has nothing to do with ordinary toddler awkwardness
- Repeatedly closing one eye or holding a hand over one eye when looking at something
- Holding objects extremely close or pushing them farther out to see

Vision Problems

There are many vision anomalies to consider if you think your toddler has a problem. Three of these—farsightedness, nearsightedness, and astigmatism—are well recognized.

Farsightedness, which is often inherited, means your toddler has trouble seeing things up close. All babies start out farsighted, but vision usually corrects itself over time. Farsightedness is not considered a problem unless it does not go away later in the child's life.

Nearsightedness means your toddler cannot see far in the distance. This condition can begin in toddlerhood, but most of the time it develops later. Heredity is also a factor in this condition.

Astigmatism occurs mostly with toddlers who are both nearsighted and farsighted. A toddler with astigmatism sees things in a blurred, wavy manner, and most of the time, the child will also have problems looking at things close up.

You've probably heard of "lazy eye" or "wandering eye." The medical term for this is **amblyopia**. One eye usually cannot see as well as the other, and the toddler involuntarily starts using the stronger eye, which makes the so-called "lazy eye" slow to move and see.

Although many infants appear cross-eyed at birth, this condition usually disappears during the first year. If it doesn't disappear, the problem of **strabismus** is present. Farsighted toddlers are more susceptible to this condition.

You may have seen children with droopy eyelids, the condition known as **ptosis**. Ptosis can affect one or both eyes, but it impacts vision because it basically inhibits it. Weakened muscles in the eyelids are the culprit. Unfortunately, eyeglasses don't fix this. Surgery is almost always needed and is usually done when a toddler is three to four years old.

If your toddler needs glasses, make it a low-key affair. Find an optometrist who works specifically with children and is aware of the special challenges in working with them. Explain to your toddler that she will be able to see better. Show her other people who wear glasses and comment casually about how cute they look. Dr. Seuss wrote a wonderful book called *The Eye Book* that you might want to share with your toddler.

Hearing

Just because a parent says something to a toddler does not mean she is listening. That does not qualify as a hearing problem. Hearing specialists advise that the following signs may indicate a hearing problem:

- No response or lessened response to external stimuli
- Inability to hear very low sounds
- Consistently having no reaction when spoken to
- Inability to hear things coming from beside or behind her
- Lack of reaction to music or other noise "stimulators"
- Answering a question with a response that indicates your toddler didn't hear (For example, she responds to "Are you ready for your bath?" with "No, I'm not tired.")
- Inability to follow directions that are generally within the norm for a toddler
- Limited speech

Hearing Problems

A number of medical conditions can affect your toddler's hearing. Recurring ear infections and exposure to excessively loud noise can result in hearing problems. Some hearing loss is hereditary. If your child was exposed to viral infections while you were pregnant, there may be an increased risk for hearing problems. If your toddler experienced seizures, oxygen deprivation, or bleeding on the brain as a newborn, hearing could be affected, too. Franconi syndrome is a ringing in the ears; although it is rare, it can affect hearing, as well.

The good news about hearing is that even the tiniest problem can usually be helped with some sort of treatment. Get a thorough exam for your toddler, and if she has a hearing problem, address it immediately. The sooner you do, the smaller the effect will be on her development and functioning.

Hyperactivity

You have likely heard of attention deficit hyperactivity disorder (ADHD). It is a popular label used today both for children who are truly suffering from it and also with kids who are simply troublesome in some other way. Basically ADHD is a disorder that causes inattention, impulsiveness, and hyperactivity. All three categories can be present, or they can exist separately; they are generally present before the age of seven.

ADHD is a bit of a misnomer because these children do not suffer from a deficit of attention at all! Rather, an ADHD child's brain is bombarded with so much stimuli that his brain can't focus on just one piece of information; he is *overloaded* with information and can't decide where to place his attention. This may account for why ADHD kids appear as if they are not listening and are often described as "daydreamers."

According to the *Diagnostic and Statistical Manual-IV*, which professionals use to diagnose illnesses, inattention manifests itself through:

- failing to give close attention to details or carelessness in school, home, or other activities;
- difficulty paying attention or sustaining attention;
- not seeming to listen when spoken to directly;
- failure to follow through on activities, chores, and schoolwork;
- difficulties with organization;
- dislike, hesitance, refusal, or avoidance of activities that require sustained attention;
- losing things often;
- easy distraction by extraneous stimuli;
- frequent forgetfulness.

Impulsiveness includes often blurting out answers before questions have been completed; often demonstrating difficulty waiting for his turn; and often interrupting or intruding on others (for example, butting into conversations or games).

For a child to be diagnosed with ADHD of the inattentive type, six or more characteristics of inattentiveness have to be present for at least six months to a degree that is considered maladaptive and not consistent with a child's developmental level. For a child to be characterized as having "hyperactivity with impulsiveness," six or more of those symptoms have to be present in the same way.

Too often we don't recognize or emphasize the positive attributes of ADHD. Although they are often characterized negatively, children with ADHD are typically very bright and creative and have much to offer the world. Helping a child understand this and helping him develop his own unique talents will reduce symptoms of depression significantly.

> It is often hard to distinguish between normal physical activity in a child and hyperactivity. A hyperactive toddler is almost constantly fidgeting with his hands or feet or is generally squirmy. When remaining in his seat is expected, he gets up and can't seem to stay put. He is excessively talkative and has difficulty playing quietly. He is usually described as "always on the go" and "into everything."

Depression

About a third of children with ADHD have depression. In fact, depression is thought to affect up to 1 percent of preschoolers. Because this can be such a devastating experience, you should understand how depression can manifest itself in your toddler.

Diagnosing Depression

The *DSM-IV* lists the following symptoms necessary for a diagnosis (this list is mainly for adults):

"A. Five or more of the following symptoms have been present during the same two-week period and represent a change from previous functioning; at least one of the symptoms is either (1) depressed mood or (2) loss of interest or pleasure.

1. Depressed mood most of the day, nearly every day, as indicated by either subjective reports or observations made by others. Note: In children, it can be irritable mood.
2. Markedly diminished interest or pleasure in all, or almost all activities most of the day, nearly every day (as indicated by either subjective account or observation made by others).
3. Significant weight loss when not dieting or weight gain (e.g., a change of more than five percent of body weight within a month), or decrease or increase in appetite nearly every day. Note: In children, consider failure to make expected weight gains.
4. Insomnia (sleeplessness) or hypersomnia (getting too much sleep) nearly every day.
5. Psychomotor agitation or retardation (slow physical movement) nearly every day (observable by others, not merely subjective feelings of restlessness or being slowed down).
6. Fatigue or loss of energy nearly every day.
7. Feelings or worthlessness or excessive or inappropriate guilt (which may be delusional) nearly every day (not merely self-reproach or guilt about not being sick).
8. Diminished ability to think or concentrate, or indecisiveness, nearly every day (either by subjective account or as observed by others).
9. Recurrent thoughts of death (not just fear of dying), recurrent suicidal ideation (thoughts) without a specific plan, or a suicidal attempt or a specific plan for committing suicide.

B. The symptoms do not meet the criteria for mixed episode (of depression and mania).

C. The symptoms cause clinically significant distress or impairment in social, occupational, or other important areas of functioning.

D. The symptoms are not due to the direct physiological effects of a substance (e.g., a drug of abuse, a medication) or a general medical condition (like hypothyroidism).

E. The symptoms are not better accounted for by bereavement, such as the loss of a loved one, the symptoms persist for longer than two months or are characterized by marked functional impairment, morbid preoccupation with worthlessness, suicidal ideation, psychotic symptoms, or psychomotor retardation."

You'll notice that children were mentioned only twice in this description of depressive symptoms. Although it is important for you to understand the clinical definition of depression, you'll have to look very carefully at your toddler for specific signs of depression.

Depression or Sadness?

How do you figure out if your toddler is depressed instead of just sad? The biggest thing to watch for is whether the symptoms you are observing are causing a substantial amount of interference in his day-to-day functioning. Depression in children does not always follow the two-week rule in which the symptoms have to be present constantly. In kids, the symptoms can come and go, but watch for them to frequently pop up over that time frame.

Another way to see whether your toddler is just in a funk or really depressed is to take the HALT test. Ask these questions about your child.

- Is he <u>H</u>ungry?
- Is he <u>A</u>ngry?

- Is he <u>L</u>onely?
- Is he <u>T</u>ired?

If the answer is yes to any of these, he may just have a temporary case of the blues. Easy ways to treat the blues are for your child to grab a snack, get some exercise, or lie down for a nap.

Symptoms of depression fall into two categories: behavioral and emotional. What follows is a more general explanation of symptoms in toddlers. As you read about them, you will begin to see just how hard it is to make an accurate diagnosis of depression in toddlers.

Behavioral Symptoms of Depression

At a glance, the following are behavioral symptoms of depressed children under the age of three: feeding problems; tantrums; and lack of emotional expression. Between ages three and four: fears; enuresis or encopresis (incontinence); frequent crying and oversensitivity; lack of interest in others, including children; and decreased attention and increased distractibility.

Before the age of three, there are a few problems to watch out for. Feeding problems are typical with toddlers who are depressed. With babies and very young children, there is a failure to thrive, an inability to "keep up" with the changes in normal development. Things that should interest them don't. Tantrums, in the form of constant crying, are common.

As children reach the ages of three and four, they begin "acting out" as a means of communicating what is happening to them emotionally. It is not a total surprise that a once-loved book can quickly become boring; what you're looking for is a lack of interest across the board in most activities that a child of a certain age should enjoy. Children who are generally quiet and reserved may become hyperactive, or unable to control their excessive activity. An outgoing toddler may become shy or disinterested in being around other children. He will be resistant to new activities such as attending preschool or going to a party. Previously potty-trained toddlers may begin to have accidents both during the day and at night, or they may become constipated. Often, a toddler will become less able to handle frustration.

Resist the urge to latch onto a couple of behaviors that seem to fit your child and automatically assume there is trouble brewing. These behaviors could be attributed to just about anything. Children often find a way to communicate when and how you least expect them to; with some patience and a little time, you should have your answer. Although some of these symptoms may seem normal for your child, if they are causing him significant discomfort, there is a problem.

> The symptoms of depression manifest themselves in very different ways at varying ages. It's important to remember that you are looking for signs or behaviors that are out of character for *your* child. If you find yourself thinking "He never acts like that," pay attention. His behavior does not necessarily mean he is depressed or suffering from anything extraordinary—he might just be having a rough patch—but you should keep your eye on things.

Emotional Symptoms of Depression

Emotional symptoms can also be present. Before the age of three, crying jags are an expression of anger, anxiety, or dissatisfaction. Some theorists believe that this type of crying also can be an expression of fear and insecurity. A lack of interest in others, especially other children, and little to no facial expression are also sometimes indicators of depression. Because this is an age at which emotions cannot be expressed verbally, you'll need to fine-tune your ability to interpret the body language of your child.

Between ages three and five, emotions are still expressed primarily through acting out. A toddler might refuse to go to day care or to another place that he previously couldn't wait to attend. Extreme clinginess and a refusal to interact with others also may indicate some sort of problem. You may hear about frequent tummy aches or other ailments. Some toddlers may voice vague emotional complaints, such as being sad or being scared.

If you suspect your child may be depressed, take your concerns to a professional. This diagnosis can be extremely complicated because there are so many other factors at work. Do your homework and ask for help.

Children with Special Needs

12

Becoming an Expert

Many children are born with chronic conditions that require a different pattern of care as compared with healthy children. Although some are born with these conditions, others develop them in toddlerhood. Whenever they occur, if you are the parent, you no doubt worry that your child will never have a "normal" life. Truth be told, no one can really define "normal." If what you want is to provide your child with a happy, healthy, and fulfilling life, do not let his special needs discourage you.

Once you have medical proof that your toddler does have a chronic illness, you must learn all you can about his condition. You need to know the good, the bad, and the ugly, and how your toddler will be affected. Talk to his pediatrician or specialist, find out who else needs to be a part of the treatment team, and get on it! The sooner your toddler receives the help he needs, the better off you'll all be.

For many chronic conditions, new advances are being made every day that target a cure. Get on the Internet and do your own research. (Keep in mind that not everything you read on the

Internet is true.) Even the best doctors are often too busy to read everything about every illness they treat. Take your research with you to the doctor. If your doctor finds you pesky, you are probably doing a good job! You don't want to be overly bothersome, but there is nothing wrong with being assertive. Remember, the best care for your special-needs child comes from many sources.

If possible, keep a duplicate of your child's records with you. This is more of a "just in case" precaution. You may want to get a second opinion, and having the records will make it easier. There may be an emergency with your child and no time to get the records from your doctor. Having an extra set of records will give you a sense of security.

> **Blaming yourself or being disappointed about your toddler's condition is a complete waste of time. It is what it is. Accept it, deal with it, and move on. Your toddler needs you!**

Allergies

On its face, an allergy doesn't sound like a chronic condition. But what about the kinds of allergies that make even regular, day-to-day activities dangerous? For example, food allergies or an allergic reaction to a bee sting can be life-threatening. It's scary enough to think that your toddler is vulnerable, but it's terrifying to consider that she can't just be a kid.

It is important to talk to your toddler about her serious allergy. Teach her about those things that she needs to avoid. But don't assume that you can trust her! A toddler with a food allergy, for example, is not always able to turn down something that is forbidden. She cannot understand the dangers inherent in disobeying you. Instead, be sure that whomever your toddler spends time with knows about her allergy and what should be done if there is a problem. There are ID bracelets and necklaces that you can get for your toddler to wear as an extra precaution. Never assume that someone knows how to handle an allergic reaction; unless they have had experience with the same allergy, people do not always know what to do.

As with other chronic conditions, you have to do your best to keep your child safe but you can't protect her 100 percent. She needs to be a kid, and you will have to learn to let go.

Cerebral Palsy (CP)

Although children with cerebral palsy (CP) are thought to be born with the condition, symptoms of this neuromuscular disorder don't appear until children are about six months old, and doctors usually do not make a diagnosis until the child is two to three years old. The symptoms include poor muscle control accompanied by either extremely stiff muscles or very floppy ones. Often there is developmental delay. There is no cure, but the disease is not progressive. Surgery, physical and occupational therapy, and speech training can be helpful. Intelligence does not appear to be affected, but daily life can be very difficult.

Cystic Fibrosis

The endocrine system is responsible for the secretions through the body's organs (for example, perspiration through the skin). When the endocrine system is not working properly, the secretions in a child with cystic fibrosis can fill a toddler's lungs, making it incredibly hard for him to breathe. The pancreas is affected, which causes problems with digestion. Treatment is geared toward improved nutrition, respiratory therapy, and medication. There is no cure yet, but early detection and treatment are the best protection for giving your toddler as normal a life as possible.

Diabetes

There are two types of diabetes (type 1 and type 2). The more serious type, type 1, can result in serious physical complications if it isn't treated and monitored very carefully. Type 1 diabetes is insulin dependent. Insulin is needed to convert sugar to energy before it travels to the cells. If this doesn't work, sugar builds up in the blood, and the cells don't get the energy they need. The cells start to burn fat for energy, which can cause problems, including, in the extreme, a diabetic coma.

Toddlers with type 1 diabetes have symptoms that include excessive urination and thirst, a very big appetite with little or no weight gain, and lethargy. Treatment includes insulin injections coupled with dietary restrictions and monitoring of glucose levels. Toddlers do not enjoy the injections, as you can well imagine. You should educate your toddler early and help her to understand that her treatment is crucial in remaining healthy. Diabetes need not be crippling, but it will require careful, frequent, and consistent monitoring to keep your toddler as healthy as possible.

Cancer

Although it is a rare occurrence, cancer can strike toddlers. The word *cancer* can paralyze a parent with fear and a sense of helplessness. Many of us immediately assume that a child with cancer can't have a childhood, but this isn't true.

The treatments for cancer are steadily improving, and we may even see a cure within our lifetimes. Until then, if your toddler has cancer, early detection and treatment are key. Anyone who has had cancer or knows someone with cancer will tell you that psychological treatment is just as important as the physical treatment.

You and your toddler will need help accepting your child's diagnosis, and education is the first way to calm fear. You will also need to help your toddler deal with her questions, her fears, and her treatments. She needs to be able to express her feelings, whether she can do so verbally or not. She needs to see you being strong and proactive. The example you set for her will be invaluable in helping her to fight her illness.

Down Syndrome

Some children are born with Down syndrome, and there is no cure. Most people assume that mental retardation is a part of this disorder, and that is true for the most part, but some children with Down syndrome have normal intelligence. Sometimes therapy can advance the IQ into the normal range in children who are treated early; most, however, have some sort of impairment that makes independent living later in life difficult.

Children with Down syndrome are known to be affectionate, kind, and sensitive. Other children can be cruel, and children with Down syndrome are an easy target for ridicule and are sometimes made the butt of jokes. It may help to find other families with a Down's child so that your toddler can associate with someone who knows what it's like to be "different." You cannot protect your child from the comments and attention of others, however; and you would be doing him a disservice in keeping him hidden away. Your Down's child is special; and it will be up to you to show him how very special he is.

Autism

If you hear the diagnosis *autism*, you may be terrified. It is a scary diagnosis, to be sure, and it requires a thorough understanding of symptoms and treatments. Autism is probably one of the most challenging and difficult disorders to treat, but progress can be made.

Autism is considered to be a pervasive developmental condition that can include any or all of the following symptoms:

- Very poor verbal communication with limited ability to initiate conversations
- Very limited or poor eye contact with others
- Poor social skills
- Little to no facial expressions
- Very restricted interests
- Screaming, head banging, biting, scratching
- Seeming to have no affection for anyone
- Appearing very unhappy and unreachable
- Often focusing on one thing that the child cannot seem to let go
- Not showing a lot of interest in toys or other children
- Often gifted, but mislabeled as mentally retarded

There are more symptoms, but autism is a diagnosis that needs to be made slowly and with careful consideration. Treatment consists of a comprehensive approach, often involving social skills development, language therapy, counseling, special education programs when necessary, and medication. A professional specialist who is trained in treating autism is key to making progress with autistic kids.

Mental Retardation

Toddlers with mental retardation can suffer from milder forms to more pervasive, severe forms of the condition. Mental retardation affects the ability to learn and can make the formation of relationships difficult. Mild retardation may affect language, motor skills, emotion, and cognition. As the level of retardation increases, the deficits become more serious. As with the other illnesses discussed here, early detection is crucial.

Other Special Needs

There are other illnesses that create special needs for a child: epilepsy, asthma, hearing and vision impairments, juvenile rheumatoid arthritis, muscular dystrophy, and AIDS.

Many sources of help and information are available to you if your toddler has a disabling condition; you can find a list in the Resources section at the end of the book. One such resource is IDEA—the Individuals with Disabilities Education Act. This law helps parents to seek help, treatment, special programs, and services for children with special needs. It also promises access to public spaces, public transportation, and public resources so that your child can have as many opportunities as possible.

Discovering that your toddler is a child with special needs can certainly be heartbreaking. Allow yourself time to grieve, but don't let yourself drown in self-pity and obsessive worrying. Your toddler is going to need you more than ever, and you are embarking on a rough journey. There will be hard times, no doubt, but there will also be good times and great moments. You may have to live differently from other families, but your life doesn't have to be unhappy. Children with special needs seem to have unique gifts, and once we are able to overlook their impairments, we will be able to see their assets and the joy they bring to life.

13

Socialization

Fostering Relationships outside the Immediate Family

Toddlers are busy little beings. They are learning all sorts of new things, and often they are learning so quickly that it's hard for the rest of us to keep up. In addition, they are beginning to interact with others, forming close bonds with close family members. Experts agree that we learn much about relationships through the first relationships we have as children.

Extended Family and Close Friends

Including the extended family and other close friends in your toddler's life is one of the best gifts you can give. Parents can get caught up in the day-to-day rearing of children, and they sometimes overlook the relationship needs of a child. A parent cannot provide 100 percent of a child's needs. In a two-parent family, often the mother has strengths that the father doesn't and vice versa. Between the two of them, they can generally meet most of their child's needs, but allowing close family and friends to help ensures that additional needs will be met as well.

What you are offering during this time is the opportunity to observe social skills and to imitate them. Your toddler is likely to mimic the attributes of family members and friends that you find appealing.

Being part of a family is the toddler's first brush with socialization. Her social skills are learned, not natural. It will be up to you to teach her how to play and interact with others. Because much of the way she learns is through observation, the way you interact with others will be closely watched. All of your relationships have the ability to impart something useful to your toddler.

Spoiling Toddlers

Extended family—grandparents, aunts, uncles, and cousins—are invaluable. They love your child like no one else will, often believing that your little angel is perfect despite evidence to the contrary! Is it alright if these individuals spoil your toddler? Yes, and no. All children need people in their lives who think they hung the moon; being spoiled goes along with that. But there are two ways to "spoil" a child. The first is to give a child everything she wants, and when she misbehaves, do nothing about it but insist that she is fine. This child will probably turn into a spoiled brat. She will learn to have no regard for others and their feelings, and she will expect everyone, not just her family, to treat her in the same way. She comes to truly believe the world revolves around her.

The second kind of spoiled child is the one who is treated like she hung the moon by her grandparents or other adults in her life. She is showered with gifts and fun times. The difference is this: when she does something wrong, her loved ones are able to separate the acts from the child. She is punished, and she is expected to take responsibility. Parents often blame a child's wrongdoing on themselves, as if their child's misbehavior is a reflection on them.

Grandparents, aunts, and uncles are removed enough that they don't take a child's misdeeds so personally. What a wonderful gift to give a toddler—security in her relatives' love and acceptance.

Learning to Play Nice

How do you help a toddler develop the skills necessary to form good, solid relationships and interactions? Aside from the family, one of the first places a toddler has exposure to other children is through playtime and play dates with other toddlers. Some toddlers are overwhelmed by a bigger group of children, so play dates are a perfect place to start.

Play Dates

When arranging a play date, keep your expectations low. You are getting two toddlers together, after all, and it may not be pretty. Pick a parent and child both you and your toddler enjoy. No, it isn't *your* play date, but you will be spending time with the other parent, so you'll want to be with a person whose company you can enjoy and who thinks similarly to you. Arrange for the four of you to get together for a short amount of time. A long play date will wear the kids out, and they are bound to become cranky and irascible, which will ultimately lead to trouble. Plan the play date at a time when the children are apt to be at their best, for example, after a nap or earlier in the morning.

When you get together for the first time, don't push the children; let them get used to each other. You might have some activities placed out in the room—crayons, toys, and stuffed animals—that are ready for play should the toddlers be interested. Don't hover but let them know that you are nearby if you are needed.

Try not to intervene at the first sign of trouble. As long as the toddlers are not hurting each other, try to let them work it out. Toddlers have short memories, and once a conflict is over, they usually become the best of friends again quickly. Make sure that you and the other parent see eye to eye on such issues so the two of you don't begin to have disagreements about the children.

Expect conflict. Sharing is not a natural behavior for toddlers. When problems with sharing occur, allow both toddlers a chance to play with the toy or try to divert the attention of one to another activity. When nothing works, take the toy away and get them involved in something else. If a lot of crying and arguing persists, it's perfectly okay to cut the play date short and schedule another time.

Play Groups

The next step up in toddler socialization is the play group, with three to four children playing together. Other group situations that can be beneficial are Mother's Day Out programs, day care, "Mommy and Me" classes, and other out-of-the-home activities. These activities allow a toddler to interact with several children and learn to navigate relationships. As with a play date, there will be problems and conflicts, but this is part of the learning process. Find out how the supervisor of these activities plans to handle conflict and back that person up if you can. In other words, do not let your toddler think he can misbehave with this individual or that you will necessarily take up for him in a dispute.

Your Child's Personality

Some children are gregarious, boisterous, and outgoing. Others are naturally shy, reticent, and cautious. Respect your child's personality and don't try to make him someone he is not. If he loves to be with others, allow him opportunities to do so. If he is uncomfortable, he may prefer being with only one or two children. This does not mean he will become a loner or he will have terrible relationships. Follow your child's lead as to how much stimulation he can tolerate. The goal is to have successful interactions; tailor the interactions so that he enjoys them rather than becoming anxious in the face of them.

Tantrums

There's nothing more fun than being able to get out of the house and taking your toddler with you to enjoy new experiences. And then there's the not-so-fun part—the tantrums.

Toddlers have tantrums for several reasons. The most obvious one is the need to express frustration or some other emotion. Toddlers cannot always verbalize what they are feeling inside, so they act out. A tantrum says, "I'm mad, and I can't take it anymore!" If you've ever witnessed a tantrum, you know this sort of behavior gets noticed!

Some toddlers cannot handle frustration when they are hungry, tired, or overwhelmed by stimulation. Like adults, whatever is happening is simply *too much* when their level of tolerance is negatively affected. Other toddlers have tantrums when they feel they have no control over what is happening. Sounds familiar, right? Feeling helpless and unable to meet the demands of a situation leads to uncharacteristic behavior.

If you can, prepare for tantrums. If you are planning to take your toddler out, do it at a time when he is the most rested, well fed, and least frustrated. Carry snacks or a small toy to keep your toddler entertained. Boredom breeds discontent, and discontent leads to

Lest you forget, none of us are immune to those bursts of frustration and anger. If you are honest, think back to the last time you became highly upset about something—the traffic, the line in the grocery store, your supervisor's demands, the breaking of the washing machine—you get the point. If these things can drive you to have a full-blown tantrum, imagine how a toddler feels when he has no control over something that happens to him.

tantrums. Keep your outings short if possible. Don't take a toddler to a restaurant that doesn't tolerate children well. If you must, go early and take entertainment in the form of a quiet toy or book.

Techniques for Tantrums

There is no magic wand for stopping a tantrum, but are there some useful techniques? Yes. The first is to remove your toddler from the situation. This is not the time to teach your toddler a lesson in handling her frustration. You also need to forget trying to reason with her. Once anyone is that upset, it's hard for them to calm down and think rationally.

Try distracting your toddler. Sometimes this works, and at other times, it can make the tantrum worse. Whatever you do, stay calm. There is no reason to respond with punishment. All you will accomplish is an increase in her frustration and an even worse tantrum.

It's okay to say something to your toddler that lets her know you understand her frustration. If you are in a store, for example, and she wants everything she sees, you might tell her, "I know you are angry right now. You can't have everything you want, and I hate that, too. Let's sit here for a minute and calm ourselves down." Will it work? Maybe, maybe not.

Can you ignore her tantrum? Yes, but it takes a lot of strength. Your first impulse is to quiet her down, particularly when others are watching the two of you. Do not give in to embarrassment because your toddler will smell the humiliation on you!

> **Although your toddler's antics during a tantrum may seem cute or funny, resist the urge to laugh or to dismiss her. Think about how you feel when you are having a tantrum. A tantrum is an expression of uncomfortable emotion; it's not an act. Laughing can cause your toddler to react even more strongly.**

She will pull this on you again once she knows. As long as your toddler is not hurting herself (by banging her head, for example), let her have her tantrum. If you wish, physically pick her up, take her to the car, and let her finish the tantrum there.

You've figured out by now that handling and stopping a tantrum is really a roll of the dice. Just when you think you *have* figured out the best way to manage her tantrums, it won't work the next time! Whatever you do, don't be hard on yourself. Tantrums are a normal part of life for toddlers—and for their parents, too.

Fostering Good Table Manners

As discussed before, learning good table manners is a work in progress. Your toddler may be able to put her napkin in her lap, but may not remember to use it. She will watch what you are doing, even though she may not model it. A toddler with good manners is really a fantasy! After all, they are learning to handle food, eat, master utensils, and get the food in their mouths rather than all over themselves. As toddlers learn to eat with utensils, you should expect a mess. She just wants to eat—she really doesn't care how she looks.

Practicing Good Manners

If you want success as you begin to take your toddler out to eat in public, start by practicing at home. Play up the meal and how your toddler gets to be a "big girl." Let her help you set the table. Get her a spoon and fork that fit her little hands. Or you might try having a "tea party" where you can model good table manners for her.

As with tantrums, do not laugh when your toddler makes a mess with her dinner. Instead, put only a few items on her plate so you don't overwhelm her. If she throws food on the floor, ignore her. If you can't, tell her that throwing food isn't done by big girls and move on. Again, keep your reaction low-key so she doesn't sense your frustration or bemusement and do it again to get your attention.

Reasonable Expectations

What is reasonable to expect in terms of table manners with a toddler? She should be able to handle a spoon and fork, albeit clumsily. (It is better if they are child-sized utensils.) She should be able to say "please" and "thank you." She should be able to put her napkin in her lap, but she won't really see the point in leaving it there. She cannot tolerate a lot of boredom, so time your meals so that she doesn't have to sit still for very long. She should also be able to ask to be excused.

Focus on letting toddlers have new responsibilities. A three- or four-year-old is capable of putting his clothes in the drawer, of sweeping the floor (with a kid-sized broom.), and helping to gather the trash. Find tasks that are age- and ability-appropriate. The focus should be on letting him feel a sense of mastery and control over his world.

If you are a person who prizes good manners, you are probably going to be disappointed at first. The more you try to force her to conform to your high standards, the more likely she is to resist. Save the etiquette lessons for later. If you can teach her a few basics, you will have succeeded!

Teaching Responsibility

Toddlers are much more concerned about themselves than anyone else, but part of being a responsible person includes the ability to understand how your behavior affects others. Toddlers see responsibility as merely an opportunity to learn to do things themselves and to assert their independence.

The tasks he is given will probably not be done perfectly, but you need to pick your battles. Is it more important to have the clothes perfectly placed in the drawer and the dust completely swept up or to help your toddler with his development? It is easy for any of us to get caught up in wanting things to be done neatly and well. After all, who wants to go behind someone and clean up after them? But the tasks that your toddler is doing are not meant to teach him neatness or perfection. He wants to show himself—and you—that he is independent and competent. Letting him handle responsibility allows him to do just that.

"Outwitting" Your Toddler

Toddlers have a special knack for turning us into idiots. Just when we think we are grown-ups with the knowledge of how to handle just about anything that life throws us, a toddler can do something that leaves us feeling completely baffled. Toddlers can make us question our abilities, our intelligence, and our behaviors.

You are no different from any other parent of a toddler. A toddler's job is to learn, develop her personality, and test her limits. And the lucky recipient of most of her antics is her parent! It is perfectly normal for you to wonder what will happen next, and you may begin to think you will never get control over your life.

Anticipate and Plan Ahead

The key is anticipating the good and the bad and planning ahead for problems as well as good times. Think about your toddler's strengths and play up to them. For example, if she shines when she is rested, take her out only when she is rested. If she is really good at creative endeavors, let her succeed in and share her talent. Think about her weaknesses. If she is shy, don't force her to be the center of attention at a gathering. If she is not very coordinated, don't make her play a game of ball. In other words, help build her confidence by letting her shine at the things she naturally does well.

If you expect your toddler to react negatively to a particular situation, anticipate that and find a way to avoid it. If you can't do that, then try to arrange things so that your toddler doesn't become frustrated or upset. It may sound as if you are being asked to be overprotective and never let your child experience anything bad; that is partly true and partly not true.

Outwitting your toddler doesn't mean that you don't let your toddler learn certain lessons from negative experiences. It does mean not letting innocent distractions cause interruptions in your toddler's life. She needs to have as many successes as possible, and at times, she needs your intervention to make that happen. She doesn't need to be humiliated or embarrassed. Contrary to popular belief, nothing good comes out of that! Outwitting your toddler ensures that she will come to see herself in a positive, honest light, and you will be instrumental in that journey.

14

Parenting without Guilt

Normal Feelings about Parenting

This author conducted an informal survey of 20 parents to see how they *really* feel about parenting. It was done in order to emphasize that it is perfectly okay to have negative feelings about what has been called the greatest job of all.

What is the Best Part of Being a Parent?

"I get the chance to influence a human life, to teach him, and to mold him into a happy adult."

"I get the biggest kick out of watching my twins learn new things. Their curiosity is incredible. I hope they don't lose that."

"I am doing something that is outside of myself, know what I mean? Parenting requires that my focus be entirely on someone else."

"It's the love I get in return—there's nothing like it."

What's the Worst Part of Being a Parent?

"The job never ends! It's like I am on call 24 hours a day, 365 days a year."

"Nobody seems to appreciate what I do."

"Being a parent keeps me worried all the time. Am I doing it right? Is my child healthy? Is she happy? Will she be smart?"

"No freedom, or I have to plan for freedom—I have lost my spontaneity!"

"I feel like someone is tapping my shoulder all the time, saying, 'Mommy, Mommy, Mommy.' It's maddening!"

"I feel guilty all the time—that I'm not doing enough or that I am smothering her. Am I spending enough time with her? Is my job suffering?"

Would You Do It All Over Again?

"Absolutely!"

"Absolutely not!"

This mini-survey is nothing scholarly, but you probably recognize yourself in at least some of those statements. Society has taught us to believe that parenthood is the end all, be all of life. For some, it is, but for others, this is just not the case. Rarely is your experience of having children exactly as you dreamed it would be. Parenthood for you may be so far off the mark of what you'd anticipated that you are unhappy, unfulfilled, and disappointed.

Wouldn't it be nice if it weren't such a big deal to discuss your negative feelings about parenting and your child without being thought of as a monster of sorts? Making parenting sound like a magical, euphoric experience sets us all up for disappointment because it simply isn't that way.

If you have gripes about being a parent, first accept that you are being one of the honest few who can really be truthful about your experiences. Second, share your feelings with another trusted parent who won't discount how you are feeling. Being able to talk about this is cathartic, and you will find that you are not unique in the way you feel—you simply had the guts to say it out loud!

Third, know that just because you don't always love your job as a parent this does not make you a bad parent. In fact, acknowledging that parenting isn't always all it's cracked up to be puts you in a much more realistic place in terms of your expectations of yourself and your child.

Developing Your Own Brand of Discipline

If there were only one way to discipline a child, we wouldn't see all those how-to books on discipline on the shelves of every bookstore. We'd all discipline in the same way, and to a certain extent, we'd be trying to raise kids as if they were robots. What works with one toddler won't make any sense with another toddler. Often you will see this in your own home if you have more than one child.

The dictionary defines discipline as "training intended to produce a specified character or pattern of behavior." It also defines it as "punishment." But discipline should not be intended to be punishment alone. You are disciplining your child so that he is able to function as a responsible, ethical person. The world beyond your home has rules and limits, doesn't it? You cannot always do what you wish as a grown-up, and children must learn this as well or face great difficulties as they grow older.

There are some things you need to keep in mind when forming your arsenal of disciplining techniques.

> Obviously, you want and need to teach your toddler right from wrong. This includes helping him to see how his actions affect himself as well as others, but another benefit of discipline is that it engenders self-discipline later on. The limits and rules that you have in place for your toddler will teach him that he will have to do the same for himself as he gets older.

One size will not fit all.

We already know that what works for one child may not work for another. But you should also know that what works today with your toddler may not work tomorrow, so you will have to be on your toes!

This is not a contest.

You don't have to win every battle with your toddler. Do not let discipline become a point of pride for you so that you cannot give in when necessary.

Consistency is the key.

If you do not allow running in the house this morning, it shouldn't be allowed this afternoon. For discipline to be effective, it should be as consistent as possible. Occasionally it's necessary to bend a rule or suspend one, but for the most part, toddlers need to know what is expected of them. Inconsistency sends mixed messages, and a toddler learns that she can manipulate the system easily.

It's okay to make mistakes.

Toddlers learn by doing. And they can't learn if they aren't given a chance to make mistakes. We learn from doing things right, but we learn much more from those things that we mess up!

Always separate the behavior from the child.

Children are not born "bad." In fact, they have no knowledge of good versus bad until they begin to learn it. Often a toddler will look as if he is doing something wrong, but he may not even realize it. Telling a child that he is bad, rude, or irritating is not good for his self-esteem. If he hears that too often, that is how he will begin to see himself.

Making Rules

Rules are designed to control and mold behavior and generally to protect your toddler from harm. They are guidelines for creating structure for your toddler, something he needs desperately. Knowing what he can and cannot do gives him a feeling of security. He knows what to expect, and life is not as overwhelming. So how do you set rules?

Will "Too Many" Rules Backfire?

A toddler's memory is short, so having a rule for everything is setting him up for failure. Pick one to three things that are important and make rules about them. For example, if you want to reinforce the habit of picking up toys and using an "indoor voice" at the dinner table, the rules may go something like this: "When you play with your toys in the den, you will need to pick them up when you are finished." And, "At the dinner table, only indoor voices are allowed." An ineffective way to word these rules would be: "You are making a mess. Clean that up before I get mad." And, "Quit screaming like a hyena. We can all hear you!"

You should be setting short, simple rules that are positive in tone and do not characterize your toddler as "bad." Your toddler may not remember even two rules, but when reminded, she will get the point. When deciding what to make rules about, find behaviors that are troublesome and concentrate on those. Not everything needs to be controlled or corrected.

Dealing with Absolutes

Should you try to make rules that include the words "don't" and "never?" If you do, you are setting yourself up for having to live under absolute rules or give in, and neither is reasonable. The words "don't" and "never" should be saved only for rules that are meant to protect your toddler from harm, such as "Don't ever get into a pool when Mommy or Daddy is not watching you," or "Never touch the hot stove." Those are rules that you won't have to give into.

Picking Your Battles

Is it more important for your toddler to have limits about picking up his toys or using an inside voice? If both are important, fine. But there's no need to have a rule about *everything*. Your toddler needs room to wiggle, experiment, and learn. Having too many rules will only encourage rebellion and resistance.

Flexibility

Remain flexible. If what you're doing isn't working, try something else. Be flexible and willing to change your rules—but not your fundamental values—to fit your unique child.

Picking Your Punishment

There are many discipline techniques to pick from, and we'll just explore a few. If these don't fit your needs, you may need to do some research on your own.

1-2-3 Magic

One of the most popular techniques around today is called "1-2-3 Magic." It was developed by Dr. Thomas Phelan and is so easy that anyone can do it. It's pretty effective for smaller children, but the key to making it work is consistency. First, you choose a behavior you wish to control, such as picking up toys before bedtime. Give your toddler the rule; for example, "Before you go to bed, you must pick up your toys and put them in your toy box. If you don't, I will count to three, and if you still haven't done it, we won't read a story together before bed."

When bedtime arrives, remind your toddler of the rule. "John, it's time to put away your toys before bed." If he ignores you, say out loud, "One," and wait about 15 to 30 seconds (remember, toddlers have little concept of time, so the sooner you move along the better). If he is not putting away his toys yet, say, "Two." Wait again for 15 to 30 seconds. "Three" is his last chance, and if he still isn't complying, it is time to say, "Okay, that's it. Let's put on your pajamas and get into bed, but we won't be reading a story tonight." Of course, he will ask, "Why?" Repeat the rule and explain that you counted and he didn't obey, so there will be consequences.

Notice that you should not force him to put up his toys *after* he disobeys you. There's a good reason for that. Forcing him to pick up his toys after he has not complied with the rule sends two messages: first, the rule doesn't have to be followed, and second, your toddler will wonder, "If I do it now, why can't I have my story?" Although the goal of the rule is to get him to clean up after playing, the object of the discipline is helping him learn there are rules and consequences. Don't sacrifice the larger goal of teaching discipline for the smaller goal of a neat room.

Timeouts

Timeouts are also a widely used discipline technique. When a toddler misbehaves or breaks a rule, his punishment is a "timeout," which really is better phrased as "time away." The toddler is removed from the situation and placed where there is no reinforcement available for his bad behavior. Were you ever put in the corner when you were a child? This is much the same. Some parents have a designated timeout chair that is used only for this purpose. Some send a child to his room, although this practice is not recommended if you want him to see his room as a pleasant place and one that he wants to go to. Just as you would do with 1-2-3 Magic, tell your toddler ahead of time which behaviors will warrant a timeout. Do not surprise him by telling him to go to timeout when he does something you don't like. He won't understand.

Pick a specific amount of time that your toddler will be in time-out. It's usually a good idea to use a minute for each year in age. For example, a three-year-old would be in timeout for three minutes. Set a kitchen timer for three minutes so that the toddler can hear an alarm that lets him know he is allowed to rejoin you. Think three minutes sounds too short? It may sound like it, but for a toddler, it is an eternity! Why make him more frustrated by having him sit still for longer than he is able?

Wherever you decide to put your toddler in timeout, make sure that you are out of earshot and sight. Toddlers like attention, even if it's negative attention. Prevent him from getting any unwitting reinforcement from you. He will likely cry and beg for you, but you will have to ignore it.

What if he refuses to stay in timeout? Experts disagree about the best way to handle this. Some say you should take him back and force him to stay, even holding him down if necessary or locking the door. If you do this, however, you are both giving him attention and frustrating him more than is necessary. Others say that if a child refuses to go into timeout, you should choose an alternate form of discipline for that child. Some children are just not cooperative, and this method won't work.

A middle-of-the-road approach is probably best for timeouts. If your toddler refuses to go into timeout or leaves it prematurely, take him firmly by the hand and walk him to his timeout spot. If he remains for the entire time, praise him. It may take several tries at first because he will test you to see if you will give in. If you are consistent and have tried faithfully but it still isn't working, find another way to discipline!

Rewarding Good Behavior

Although this seems obvious, rewarding good behavior is an excellent technique to use with toddlers. We tend to spend much more time noticing the bad things children do than the good things. When children are being good, we often overlook it because "that is what he is *supposed* to be doing." Toddlers don't have a strong sense of good versus bad, so they really don't always know they *ought* to be doing something. When you observe your toddler doing something "good," tell him. "You were so quiet while I finished working on the computer. Thank you." As the saying goes, "You catch more flies with honey than with vinegar." With toddlers, this is so true! They love to see you happy and excited. They respond much better to that than to being scolded.

Discipline that *Doesn't* Work

We have all been guilty of yelling "Stop that right now!" from across the room. How often does it really work? Hardly ever. A toddler generally finds this type of behavior from you funny and continues doing what he wants. Rather than disciplining from afar, get close. Calmly approach him, stop what he is doing, and take his hands or hold his head in your hands. Look him in the eye and say, "You must stop throwing the ball in the house now. Do you understand?" He still may try to wiggle away and repeat the behavior at which point you may have to put him in timeout or mete out some other discipline. Just know that your screaming and threatening won't work and are generally found to be funny by a toddler.

Guilt and Unconditional Love

Using guilt and making your love conditional are two techniques that are unfair, cruel, and ineffective. No child should be made to feel responsible for your happiness. You want a toddler to follow rules because they are important, not because disobeying will upset you. When a child feels guilty or thinks you don't love him because of his behavior, he grows up to think that if he doesn't please everyone, he will not be loved.

"No!"

"No!" What a huge two-letter word! Toddlers likely hear it a lot but don't pay much attention to it. They love to say "No!" and find it to be fun. When you say it, they will usually not take you seriously and will probably mimic you by repeating "No!" When this happens, don't repeat yourself or fuss at your toddler for imitating you—the less reaction you can show, the better.

Common Questions

Here are some common questions that parenting experts get asked frequently.

Is "Because I Said So" Enough?

Parents may say, "No means no." Or, "Because I said so, that's why." You've certainly heard other parents say these things, and you may even have said them yourself. Well, in part they're true and should be enough of a reason for not doing something, but using these phrases really doesn't teach your toddler anything. Remember, you are attempting to teach the concept of appropriate behavior. A short, simple explanation is fine. Say "You cannot climb on the kitchen counter because you may fall onto the hard tiled floor." If your toddler repeats "Why?" over and over again, answer the first couple of times with the very same explanation. If he is trying to get you to change your mind and your story, he'll quickly realize it isn't working. After that, refuse to answer his "whys" by ignoring him.

What's Wrong with Bribing?

The problem with bargaining is that once you start it, your toddler expects you to bribe or bargain with him every time you want him to do something. The only time it really works is if your toddler is faced with something particularly uncomfortable, scary, or unpleasant. For example, if your toddler has a fear of the doctor and it's time for his yearly checkup and vaccinations, it may be helpful to promise that something pleasant will follow. You might say, "I know how much you dislike going to the doctor. But we have to go. Why don't we plan on having ice cream afterward?" You are not making the reward contingent on good behavior but on his going along with what needs to be done.

Will My Toddler Take Advantage of an Apology?

Apologizing for your own bad behavior or mistakes is one of the best ways to model good behavior and the acceptance of responsibility. You are not perfect, and neither is your toddler. If he makes a mistake and is told to say he's sorry, why shouldn't you be expected to do the same?

Is It Okay to Discipline Other People's Kids?

Here's a simple rule. If you are the only parent in charge (e.g., your toddler has a friend over), you have a responsibility to supervise them. If one child is harming another, step in and correct the misbehaving child. If the other parent is present, wait to let her take charge first. If she doesn't, be diplomatic. You might say, "I see the kids getting into it; we'd better stop them." Do not take sides and stay as neutral as possible.

The role of parent is not for the faint of heart. Parenting is not a skill acquired at birth—it takes persistence, hard work, and determination. You learn through a lot of trial and effort. Gather your sense of humor, try not to take yourself too seriously, and trust your gut!

15

Traveling with Your Toddler

Planning a Trip

There's nothing more fun than planning and taking a vacation or a trip to see relatives. Remember how easy it used to be when all you had to do was get yourself ready? You could organize your itinerary, pack, and be out the door in a jiffy! No more of that, my friends, now that you have a toddler!

Traveling with your toddler is much more complicated than traveling alone, and some parents don't even want to try it. You might be thinking, "I can barely make it to the mall and back with my toddler without losing my mind!" But everyone needs time away, and everyone can benefit from a vacation, even your toddler. All you really have to do is become an expert planner. Sounds simple, doesn't it? It can be if you follow these tips.

Make Your Itinerary

Although this is an obvious first step, when traveling with a toddler, preparation is even more necessary. Figure out where you want to go and what you want to do and see (more on picking the destination later). Once you have done this, cut it back by half.

The reason for this is purely to save yourself much frustration and exhaustion.

We tend to try to pack as much into a trip as possible, as if we may never have another vacation. If you've done this before, you will remember that you were madly rushing about trying to see every sight, take every tour, and make the most of the experience. You likely felt rushed and as if you could not sit down and take a break. By the end of the day, you were probably exhausted.

If you are going to travel with a toddler, take that trip and imagine trying to lug a child around at the same pace. It's enough to make your head spin, isn't it? Toddlers are notorious for putting a crimp in our plans. They won't want to do what you want to do, and they will make sure you know it! They will get cranky and tired sooner than you do. They will poop out, and nothing will be enjoyable after that.

When planning your trip, make sure there are plenty of fun things to do and plenty of downtime. Toddlers need time to unwind, play, and just be toddlers. If you schedule downtime just like you schedule the tours and visits with relatives, you'll be much more likely to have a cooperative, happy toddler. This also gives you more time to do things because being with toddlers can slow you down.

If you are going to a destination that has a lot of sightseeing attractions, it's best to plan to see about two of them a day, one in the morning and one in the afternoon. For the most part, toddlers don't care about seeing what you hope to see, and they will become restless quickly. If you absolutely cannot pass up seeing the sights, you may have to take turns with your spouse. One of you can stay with your toddler while the other takes in a tourist attraction. It's not a perfect solution, but it will be a lot less frustrating for everyone.

Pack for the Occasion

No matter how you will be getting to your destination, there are certain essentials that you must carry. Your diaper bag should contain:

- Pacifiers, bottles, or sippy cup
- A change or two of clothing
- A full day's worth of diapers
- Wipes—take much more than you think you will use because they are great for all kinds of clean-up
- A half dozen freezer bags—for those other accidents!
- Medications, including something for motion sickness
- Bandages and antibiotic ointment
- Pillows and a blanket
- A small picture or two of your toddler. Tuck this into your purse or wallet, so if he gets lost, you will have a way to help others spot him.

Childproof Your Accommodations

Take along twist ties and rubber bands to hold electrical cords and close cabinets. Take a night light, too. If you need furniture moved or removed, don't hesitate to ask; most hotels are used to such parental requests.

Don't Carry It

Rent it, buy it, or have it delivered. Unless you travel with a pack mule, you can't take everything from home that you will need. There are various services available to deliver diapers, supplies, baby food, and gear directly to where you will be staying. You may think this will be too expensive, and although there is some cost involved, it is offset by the convenience factor. The following Web sites are particularly helpful:

- www.BabiesTravelLite.com—diapers, formula, etc.
- www.go-baby.com—diapers
- www.travelingtoddler.com—gear for travel
- www.babysaway.com—rental equipment (strollers, cribs, high chairs, gates, car seats, etc.)

Pack your Sense of Humor

Besides flexibility, the other important accessory when traveling with your toddler is your sense of humor. Whatever expectations you have for your trip, lower them. Things are going to happen. Your toddler *will* get bored, cranky, and tearful. Your toddler *will* refuse to go along with your plans. In other words, your toddler *will* continue to behave like a toddler even on a trip!

Traveling by Car

Just the thought of being trapped in a car with a toddler on a trip is enough to make many parents break out in a cold sweat! Taking a road trip with a toddler is not impossible, but it *does* require a good plan.

Plan Around Naptime

If you can, try to get in as much driving as you can when your toddler is sleeping. Many parents drive in the middle of the night when it's dark and their children are asleep. Others try to leave as early in the morning as possible while their toddlers are still sleeping. If it's a short trip, you can probably get most of the drive completed during your toddler's nap.

Taking Breaks

You may prefer to get in the car, drive straight through, and get to your destination as fast as possible, but with a toddler, you'd do well to ditch that plan! A good rule is to stop every two hours. Take advantage of rest areas on the side of the road. Let your toddler spend a few minutes playing and running off some of that energy. When stopping to have a meal, try to pick a place that has a playground or is located in a mall so your toddler has a chance to stretch his legs.

Packing Essentials

A full tummy makes a happy toddler! Take bottles of water and food with you in a cooler. Pack several plastic bags or containers with a day's worth of snacks that you can easily pass to your child.

Entertainment is another packing essential. Take several tote bags filled with toys, books, and games that will keep your toddler occupied. It's also a good idea to have a series of little "surprises" to hand to your toddler at several intervals. It doesn't have to be anything elaborate, and the dollar store is a perfect place to stock up. If your toddler has a favorite stuffed animal or some other security object, by all means, take it.

If your toddler enjoys listening to stories, try audio books. If your car has a DVD player, take along your toddler's favorite videos and some new ones, too. This is not the time to adhere to your strict rule of never using the TV as your babysitter! If you don't have a DVD player in your car, you can rent one. The cost is negligible when you consider the alternative—a bored, scream-ing toddler!

Interact!

Being in the car with your toddler is a great time to visit. You can point out the sights along the road. You can take turns making up a story or a song. You can sing along with the radio. If your tod-dler is old enough, play a simpler version of "I Spy." Ask him to spot a car, a tree, a truck. If he is learning his colors, have him spot colored items like a red car, a blue house, and a black dog.

Applaud Good Behavior

When your toddler is being especially pleasant or well behaved, tell him so. Nothing encourages more good behavior than noticing it when it happens!

Traveling by Plane

Many of the same rules for traveling by car apply to traveling by plane. If you can, fly when your toddler is likely to be sleeping. For short flights, try to book a nonstop itinerary. It may cost more, but you will save yourself the hassle of tearing through an airport with a toddler to catch a connecting flight! Book your tickets early enough that you can get the seats you prefer. Print your boarding passes at home to save time and effort at the airport. Even though your toddler can usually fly for free and sit in your lap while under the age of two, you may want to buy another seat on a plane, especially if you are going to be on a long flight. You and your toddler will be more comfortable. Here are some other great tips for flying with a toddler.

Don't Carry

Getting through the airport is difficult enough without a toddler. Don't plan to carry your toddler or allow him to walk in the airport unless he is playing before a flight. Transporting your child with a stroller will save you time, aggravation, and energy. If you don't want to haul a stroller around, you may want to consider a great contraption that was invented by a flight attendant called the Ride-On-Carry-On (www.rideoncarryon.com). It attaches to your rolling carry-on bag so that your toddler can roll through the airport. It then folds easily and fits into the plane's overhead compartment. Other sites that offer good baby travel-safety products are www.BabiesRUs.com and www.BabyBungalow.com.

Toddler Canyon

Toddlers love to have their own travel bag or backpack to carry books, small games, toys, security blankets, or stuffed animals. If you have one, carry along a portable DVD player. Some flights offer in-flight rentals. Others have individually controlled, in-flight TV and movies on monitors that are set into the backs of seats.

What to Wear

Do not dress your toddler in his best clothes and expect him to be clean and fresh upon arrival. Dress him comfortably in clothes that you don't mind getting messy. You can always change when you land if necessary.

Food for Flying

Nowadays, most airlines do not serve meals on shorter flights, and snacks are limited as well. Call ahead or go online to find out what your airline's meal service is and plan accordingly. With the security measures in place at airports, you may have to purchase foods from the concessions area or shops rather than packing your own. Check with your airport to find out what is acceptable.

Ear Popping

Take chewing gum with you on the plane to reduce ear popping. If your toddler is too young for gum, give him something to chew on or let him drink from a straw. These activities encourage swallowing and release the pressure that builds up in the ears.

Toddler-Friendly Destinations

When trying to decide where to take a vacation, it's best to use the same method you use when picking a restaurant in which to dine with your toddler. Find destinations that like toddlers and even cater to them. Many resorts and vacation spots that have adult sightseeing and events also have activities for children. These places have plenty of things that toddlers can enjoy and even provide very reliable babysitting services. The following is a list of excellent Web sites specifically designed to help you plan a toddler-friendly vacation and to offer you lots of fun, too!

- www.familytravelforum.com—free advice on vacations and deals
- www.Loewshotels.com/LoewsLovesKids—offers information on 19 premier retreats
- www.Away.com
- www.ChildFriendlyTravel.com
- www.KidsVacations.com
- www.Disneyparks.com
- www.Seaworld.com
- www.Escapemaker.com—for travel in the Northeast
- www.discover-carribean-cruises.com
- www.travelzoo.com—gives the top 20 vacation deals of the moment
- www.best-family-beach-vacations.com

Travel Games for Toddlers

There are more travel games and activities than you could ever imagine. Look for activities that emphasize learning shapes, colors, and numbers. Many games incorporate all of these so that your toddler is learning more than one skill at a time. Game sets that encourage your toddler to pretend and use his imagination are another great option. Some books and games have magnetic storyboards included so that your toddler can take the featured character and "act out" stories on the board.

Look for activities that allow your toddler to draw, scribble, and even color. There are kits available that have paper, markers, pencils, and more included in one simple carrying bag. Others have magnetic surfaces that can be erased with the hand. These are great when you don't have a lot of room in your car or your luggage.

Try interactive games as well. Games with just a few pieces, such as a spinner that points to different choices for activities, go over well with toddlers. Other such toys include those that have soft, padded pieces to use for pretending and telling stories.

For even more travel fun, check out:

www.alltravelingkidsfamilyvacations.com/travelgames-toddlersbaby.html

As you can see, traveling with your toddler doesn't have to be a disaster. If you plan ahead, you'll be well prepared to handle anything that comes your way!

16

Parenting Yourself to Maintain Your Sanity

What They Don't Tell You about Being a Parent

Remember how it felt to tell everyone that you were pregnant? Your friends, family, and coworkers were thrilled for you, excited at the possibility of having a new little being in the world. You spent the pregnancy looking forward to the arrival of your new baby. You and your partner made lots of plans, fantasized about your baby's future, and probably spent a lot of money getting ready!

Now that you have been a parent for several years, you may be experiencing some feelings and attitudes that you're not always proud to admit that you have. When people ask how you are doing with a new child in the house, you feel that you're supposed to respond with, "It's the most wonderful experience in my life!" This is probably true in the general sense, but on a daily basis, you may be thinking differently. More often than not, what you are longing to tell people is that you are tired and overwhelmed, and that you have a mixture of emotions that sometimes makes you feel like quite a monster.

As we discussed in Chapter 14, being dissatisfied with the job of parenting can be a normal state of being. There are an abundance of other emotions and feelings that you may have that can make you wonder how good of a parent you are, regardless of how good you are doing.

Inadequacy

Any honest parent will tell you that he or she has had feelings of inadequacy. When trying to raise a toddler, you can imagine how this inadequacy can become even more pronounced. Your toddler is developing her own personality, and along with that, she is exhibiting behaviors that you don't always understand. You read the parenting books, listen to TV interviews, and talk to other parents, but you still can't figure out your own child. What in the world is wrong with you? The answer is very simple: nothing. No one was born knowing how to be a good parent. These abilities are not innate, and you are not expected to know everything. Determining what works best with your toddler is a long process of trial and error. Sometimes you're going to make mistakes that will make you feel foolish. On other days, you'll feel a sense of accomplishment, knowing

The important thing to remember is to not let this feeling of incompetence paralyze you. If you try something and it doesn't work, be flexible enough to try something else. There are many techniques for parenting, and although you may think you have found the perfect one for your toddler, inevitably there will come a day when it doesn't work so well. That's perfectly normal, so don't let it bother you.

that you have done a good job and that your toddler is happy. Hopefully, there will be more good days than bad, but any parent will tell you that there are periods of time in which every day seems to bring on a new, frustrating challenge.

Guilt

If you're like most of us, even when you read that word, your stomach knots up just a little. Parents have been feeling guilty for one reason or another since time began. In today's world, there are challenges and factors pulling you in so many directions that some guilty feelings are inevitable. Working parents feel guilty that they're not spending enough time at home with their toddlers. They carry a sense of guilt because they wonder whether they have focused on their careers at the expense of their children. Stay-at-home parents feel guilty if they don't spend every moment playing with their toddler, and they worry if they go have some fun of their own.

As you can see, there are about as many reasons to feel guilty as there are reasons for not feeling guilty. Perhaps the best thing you can do is to understand what the word *guilt* really means. Feeling guilty implies that you have done something wrong, and that, in the course of doing something wrong, you have hurt someone else. A feeling of remorse comes from that, as well as the feeling of wishing that you had not behaved inappropriately. Look at that definition again. How many times, as a parent, can you really say that you have done something wrong on purpose, and that you really intended to hurt your toddler? The answer is pretty obvious. Save feeling guilty for when you've actually done something wrong and have done it voluntarily. The fact that you have to work, or the fact that you choose to work, is not going to be something that ruins your child. The fact that you want some time for yourself, or that you'd rather not be around your child 24 hours a day, is not a reason for feeling guilty. As you have now begun to realize, many factors contribute to your toddler's well-being. Unfortunately, it's up to the parent to balance all of these factors, but there is rarely a good reason for you to feel guilty.

Worry

All parents worry. In fact, it seems to be a hobby for some of us. You can't raise a child and never worry. You worry if your child is smart enough, happy enough, healthy enough. You worry if your child is sick, if your child is not talking, if your child isn't making friends, and on and on. An entire book could be dedicated to what parents worry about and why they shouldn't, but what's the use? Telling a parent not to worry is like telling a toddler to sit still! The bottom line is that you *are* going to worry.

What you decide to do with all this worrying is what makes it healthy or unhealthy. If you simply cannot stop worrying about your toddler for whatever reason, you may need to ask yourself why this is happening. Do you have valid reasons for worrying, or are you just one of those parents who wants everything to be perfect? You're not alone if you desire perfection, but you are going to make yourself, and your toddler, quite miserable if you worry about everything. Worry has its place, but you do not want it to overtake your life. When you worry too much, opportunities are lost to learn new things, take risks, and experience a lot of joy. Do your best to keep your worrying in check.

Resentment

Many of you will insist that you do not resent your toddlers. Congratulations to you, Super Parents! The rest of us have to be honest with ourselves. There are times when we simply resent the presence of a child or a problem that he is presenting. Haven't you ever resented your spouse? Your coworker? Your supervisor? We all have resentments toward others, particularly if they are keeping us from doing some of the things that we want to do. Why would it be any different when we have children?

If you're feeling resentful about something your toddler is doing or preventing you from doing, try to understand what is at the bottom of your resentment. If you occasionally resent your toddler simply because there are things that you would rather be doing than catering to her, or because your toddler is causing you extra frustration and trouble, this is normal and healthy. If your resentment stems from the fact that your child is not what you had fantasized he would be before his birth, you may want to reevaluate your thinking. These types of resentments are more serious and indicate that perhaps your expectations are unreasonable. Your attitude could harm your toddler's self-esteem because feelings are difficult to keep to yourself. The simple day-to-day resentments about the limitations that life with your toddler entails are irritations and feelings that you will have to manage.

Isolation

Very often, parents of toddlers say that they feel isolated and that they lack independence. You can't always go out when you want to, nap when you'd like, or do many other things when you wish. If you're a parent who does not work outside the home, you know how isolating being at home with your toddler can sometimes become. You may have developed a routine that keeps you and your toddler home most of the time, while you take care of things in the house and supervise your toddler. By the end of the day, you may realize that the only person you've talked to all day has a vocabulary of about 50 words! By the time your spouse gets home or you finally do have some other adult contact, you may feel that you are about to explode with the excitement of being able to talk to a grown-up!

Finding other mothers or fathers who are in your

> **If you're feeling increasingly isolated, the best cure is to get out of your rut. Find places to go and things to do that you and your toddler will enjoy together.**

position will be as beneficial to you as it will be to your toddler. Neither you nor your toddler needs to exist in a vacuum that includes just the two of you.

If you are feeling a lack of independence, there are some things you can do to have a few minutes to yourself. You can ask your spouse to entertain your toddler while you do something you enjoy, like take a bath or read a book—all by yourself, imagine that! If there is no one available to watch your child, find an activity in which your toddler is interested and get her involved with it while you take some time to yourself. You will still need to be in charge and on the alert for whatever your toddler might do, but you will get a few minutes of peace and quiet.

TV as a Babysitter?

Although most of the experts will tell you that television should never be used as a babysitter, this is not a practical response. There's hardly a parent out there who has not used the TV to entertain, quiet, or keep a toddler busy for a short time. The emphasis here should be on *a short time*. Parents who plop their young ones in front of the television for hours and hours on end should be cautioned that this is not a healthy approach; however, if there is a TV show or movie that your toddler particularly likes, you may want to take advantage of that for a bit while you pay your bills, use the computer, or do some other activity that keeps you in close proximity to your toddler but does not require you to interact with her.

If you are feeling awkward or selfish about letting your toddler play alone so that you can pursue something else for yourself, you should know that you are actually doing your child a service. Toddlers need to learn to play on their own and entertain themselves. The world is not going to be at their constant beck and call to entertain and stimulate them. In fact, it's healthy to teach toddlers that mommies and daddies need quiet time, too.

Work

Working outside the home can cause a mixed bag of feelings for parents. You may work not because you like it but because you have to. Your income is vital to your family's survival, and that's just the reality of the situation. Others of you, however, may have a career that you love and work that stimulates you. You are a happier individual, and thus a better parent because you work.

In any case, every working parent faces a unique set of dilemmas. You may feel that you are missing some of the special times in your child's life, or feel guilty because you've been taught that nothing is supposed to come before you child. If you're working out of necessity, you should be proud of yourself. This is a very hard thing to do, particularly if you would rather be at home with your toddler. On the other hand, if you're a parent who works because your personal happiness depends on it, you should congratulate yourself as well. Studies show that happy parents make better parents. If you're lucky enough to be able to pursue your bliss, your toddler is going to be healthier because of it. Your life may be fuller and you may be pulled in many more directions, but your family will not suffer just because you work.

Pleasing

Some parents feel a need to please everyone in the family. You want your spouse to be happy. You want your toddler to be happy. You want the whole family to be happy. Unfortunately, no matter how hard you try, you just can't please everyone. And, with all this attempted people pleasing, how often do you find that *you* aren't happy at all, but just plain old exhausted?

There is a point at which trying to please your family is healthy. Of course, you want to provide for your child's needs and your spouse's desires, and you want your family to be as happy as possible. The problem comes when you actually believe that you can make *every* person happy *all the time*. It's just not possible! You'd have better luck scaling a telephone pole greased with petroleum jelly!

If you are one of those parents crippled by the desire to please, listen up. Set more realistic expectations for yourself. When you set unrealistic expectations for yourself, you tend to expect the same from your children. Toddlers can't please you all the time, in case you haven't noticed. The fact of the matter is that you can't please them all the time either. Just do what you can.

Unconditional Love

As children, many of us were told by Mom and Dad, "I will love you no matter what you do." Many of you probably tell your children this as well. But many parents, if they're being honest, say there are times that they don't feel like they love their child at all, when what they really mean is that they don't *like* a child's behavior. It has been mentioned several times that it is important for a parent to learn to separate a toddler's behavior from who he is. Your child is going to do many things that meet with your disapproval, but this doesn't mean that you don't love him. Unconditional love means that you love a child but you do not always condone his behavior. This is an important concept to master and incorporate into your parenting so that your child learns that being loved does not depend upon what behaviors he chooses. If a toddler feels that he is loved only because of what he does, his self-esteem will suffer.

So there will be days when you just don't like your toddler. Perhaps he has been especially disobedient, mischievous, and generally difficult. Who made the rule that you have to like your child all the time? Just as with your spouse or other people that you love, you won't always *like* them. You may be asking, "But isn't the love I feel for my child supposed to be different?" Yes and no. The love that you have for your toddler *is* different from the love you have for others in your life; however, your love is still governed by feelings that are very normal, even when it comes to your baby.

Taking Steps to Nurture the Parent

You are a grown-up, and you have tons of parental responsibilities. This does not mean that you don't need somebody to parent you. Unfortunately, sometimes the only one who can do the parenting is you. When it comes to raising toddlers, or children of any age for that matter, you are going to have to learn to manage your stress. No one leads a stress-free life, no matter what they may tell you. Every life has its ups and downs, and it is the way that you manage (or mismanage) these troublesome times that determines how stressed you feel. Many parents are so overwhelmed by the pressures of day-to-day life, in addition to parenting a toddler, that they feel they have no control. Although it is true that many things are out of our control, there are steps that you can take to *get* control.

When you are learning to parent yourself, be honest about the things that you can't control; these are not personality faults or character flaws. If something is out of your control, acknowledge it and move on. It doesn't make sense to worry about things that have not happened or that are in the control of others. You don't have to like it, but simply being able to recognize it will help you to breathe a little easier.

Diet and Exercise

Another way to parent yourself is one that we all know—exercise and diet. Although most of us don't get enough exercise or eat the right foods, it is a well-known fact that these two factors can greatly enhance our health and our ability to control stress. You do not have to become an athlete or an overzealous exerciser, nor do you have to eat perfectly 100 percent of the time. Simply try to incorporate some exercise into your daily routine. You may have to break up your exercise into smaller pieces of time so that you can fit it in, or your exercise might have to include your toddler. Take a walk with him or play a game that involves physical

You know very well that toddlers have lots of energy, so what better way to get rid of some of his energy and help you accomplish your goal than to exercise together?

exercise. Some gyms that have exercise classes also provide child care. This is a great resource and one that you should consider using. Not only will you get to exercise and have a few minutes to yourself, your toddler will get to socialize with other youngsters and have some fun, too. Another way to fit exercise into your life is to take turns with another parent for babysitting duties. You may have to get creative, but the excuse that you simply don't have enough time to exercise is really just that—an excuse!

When it comes to diet, you don't have to become a health nut. Spend a few minutes looking in your pantry and your refrigerator to see what types of healthy and not-so-healthy foods are there. The goal, of course, is to have an abundance of healthy foods and a minimum of unhealthy options. Your toddler will begin adapting his food choices from observing what you eat and what you serve the family. If fast food is your meal of choice for dinner almost every night, your toddler will come to expect it as the gold standard for dining! If you're going to cook, stick to fresh foods and things that are healthy. If you don't have time for cooking, there are many frozen vegetables and other food items that can be cooked quickly in your microwave with little effort. Likewise, many fast-food restaurants are beginning to offer healthier choices on their menus. If you must get your meals at the drive-through, pick one of these options.

Getting Organized

Getting organized and managing your time will also go a long way toward helping you maintain your peace of mind. If you feel that your time is already stretched to its limits, ask yourself what you can cut out. Most parents will immediately answer, "Nothing!" If you really think about it, this probably isn't true. Does all the laundry really have to be done today? Is your house so dirty that it has become a danger zone? Is it critical that the lawn be mowed immediately and that all the leaves get raked? This is a little like the issue of control. It's important to figure out what needs to be done for the health and well-being of your family and what the real priorities should be. One of the best ways to parent yourself is to get rid of the "ought to's", "should's", and "have to's." Although this is not always reasonable because there are things that you really have to do, there are many other things that you have just convinced yourself that you must do. In reality, if you wait a day or two to mow the lawn, no one is going to suffer. If you have not vacuumed in a week, one more day simply is not going to make a difference.

Giving Yourself a Break

Give yourself the freedom to *not* do things! Your time would be better spent with your toddler or your family enjoying quality time together rather than doing chores. If you ask most adult children, they'll say what they remember most about their childhoods is the fun they had with their parents, not how clean the house was!

Do you treat yourself as you would your best friend? How nurturing of yourself are you? One way to parent and nurture yourself is to do something just for you. Do you enjoy getting your nails done? How long has it been since you played golf? Would you enjoy a massage? Would a quiet hour at a coffee shop with a book be your idea of bliss? If so, find a way to treat yourself. There is nothing wrong with doing something good for yourself, and nurturing yourself engenders positive feelings that you can pass on to the rest of the family as well. You deserve to be treated specially, and so does your spouse. Plan a date together that does not include your toddler. Again, do not use the excuse that "there isn't enough time" to keep you from taking care of yourself.

Reasonable Expectations

We all have expectations of ourselves, our toddlers, and the world in general, but how many times have those expectations been met with disappointment? Sometimes what you expect from others and yourself is just unreasonable. Often lowering your expectations and learning to laugh can be the key to avoiding these feelings.

Here's an example. It is perfectly reasonable to teach your toddler manners and the correct behavior for going to a restaurant and to expect her to behave accordingly when you are eating out. But your toddler is, after all, just a toddler. She may know that she is supposed to use her inside voice at a restaurant, and she may know that she must remain seated until the meal is over. This doesn't mean that she's going to do it though, does it? So if you're planning to take your toddler out for a meal, it's okay to remind her of the rules associated with that.

It's also important for you to remind yourself that she probably won't meet those expectations perfectly and that you shouldn't expect her to. Acknowledging this to yourself does two things. First, it reminds you that your toddler is not going to be perfect and the odds are that she will get into some sort of trouble. Second, you are much less likely to become frustrated or disappointed when your toddler does indeed behave like a toddler.

Learning to Laugh

Along with the "lowering your expectations" rule is the concept of learning to laugh. When it comes to toddlers, there are some things that are just downright funny. Don't take everything so seriously! Learn to see the funny side of the unexpected things that your toddler does. Remember that she is not trying to intentionally upset, frustrate, or disappoint you. She is merely being a kid, and if you expect anything more, you won't be amused!

Asking for Help

Contrary to what you may think, asking for help is not a sign of weakness. We are busier today than our parents were when we were growing up. Almost all of us work, and there are many family and extended family obligations. Children are generally involved in more organized and scheduled activities than in the past, and you have likely taken on various outside responsibilities as well. Whatever the reason, sometimes you just can't do it all. So where do you go for help?

Extended Family

One answer is to get help from your extended family. If you are fortunate enough to have family members who live nearby and are willing, enlist their help with babysitting. Ask them to take your toddler for a few hours so that you can get some chores done or take a well-deserved nap. Do not assume that your family members are merely agreeing to take care of your toddler because they feel they must. Most family members enjoy spending time with their young relatives. Not only does this give you a break, it also helps your toddler develop close bonds of his own with extended family.

Play Groups

Help can also come in the form of a friend with children or a neighborhood play group. If you can join forces with other mothers who have toddlers, you have built yourself a great team. You can take turns with babysitting duties, or you can all get together for an outing with the kids in tow.

Babysitters

If you'd rather have a babysitter so you can go out on your own, start looking around. Ask your friends for the names of their babysitters. Community bulletin boards in houses of worship may provide names of reliable babysitters as well.

If you're going to hire a babysitter, invite her over before you plan to go out. Have her come in on a day when you'll still be around and just let her play with your toddler while you take care of things around the house. This gives your toddler the opportunity to get comfortable with the babysitter, so that when you leave, it will not be a dramatic event. It also gives you the chance to observe how the babysitter interacts with your toddler to see if they are a good fit. Do not hesitate to ask questions such as how often she babysits, what are the ages of the children she cares for, and what sorts of activities she does with them. You can ask for references if you wish, and no babysitter should be insulted if you do.

> You might consider organized play groups and "Mother's Day Out" programs offered by churches. Utilizing these resources gives you time to take care of your own needs while your toddler is being actively entertained.

Other Parents

Sometimes help is just a supportive shoulder and an ear to listen. It's often very helpful to discuss your concerns, questions, and feelings with someone else. If you know other parents who are raising toddlers, share what is going on and ask for feedback. Other parents are some of the best sources of advice and information you can get, and a parent who has already raised a toddler can reassure you that toddlerhood does not last forever. They usually have much more of a sense of humor about this time of life because it is over for them. Sometimes they can even remind you of all the reasons that this is a very special time because they are missing it.

The Internet

Another source of support and help is the Internet. There are many parenting groups online as well as chat rooms where you can ask questions and offer opinions. Although this may be your preferred choice because of time constraints, try not to make it the only place that you seek the company of other parents. You really do need face-to-face interaction with others who are going through what you are experiencing.

Some parents find the stress and the pressures of parenting to be so overwhelming that they seek professional help. If you need help, do not be embarrassed. There are plenty of counselors who can be very useful in helping you to sort out your feelings, concerns, and conflicts when it comes to parenting your toddler. The counselor's office is a great place to be able to speak your mind without any fear of repercussions or judgment.

Whatever help you may choose to seek, don't let yourself be inhibited by the feeling that you should be able to do it all yourself. Unless you're wearing a red cape and your name happens to be Superman, there's no reason to think that you have to conquer your world all alone!

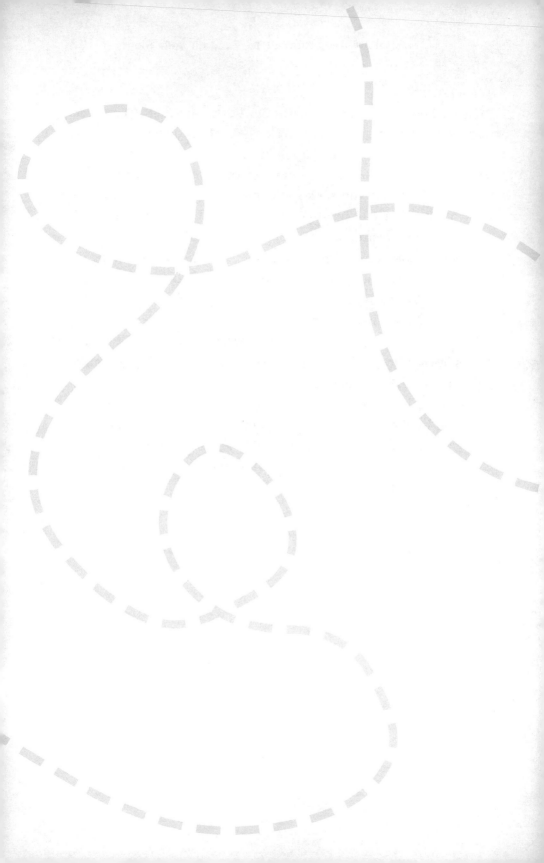

17

Getting Ready for Preschool

Is My Toddler Ready?

There is a lot of emphasis today on getting your toddler ready for school. The media, other parents, and the education system may convince you that your toddler should be educated at an earlier and earlier age. You may be surprised to learn that a child who attends preschool is not necessarily better prepared for kindergarten than a child who does not. Although it may give him a bit of an edge at first, it usually does not last long. There are certain advantages to preschool, however, that you should think about if you're considering sending your toddler. Your child will have the opportunity to interact with other toddlers, something he may not get to do regularly at home. He will also be exposed to different types of people and new activities that will create many opportunities for him to learn new things and master new skills.

Preschool Blues

Preschool should really focus on play, although other learning activities are almost always included. Your toddler may learn some basics such as her ABCs, counting, and other skills that will educate

Deciding whether your toddler is ready for pre-school is a highly individualized choice—one you'll have to make based on the needs and personality of your own child.

her about responsibility. You should think hard before allowing your child to attend a preschool that pushes any harder than this. There is simply no reason to put your toddler under so much pressure that preschool becomes something she dreads rather than looks forward to. You want preschool to be a positive experience that will translate into anticipation about attending kindergarten. The other benefit of preschool is that you get some breaks from your toddler, and there is certainly nothing wrong with that!

Is Your Toddler Ready?

It's hard to tell if your toddler is actually ready for preschool because readiness includes many factors, including your toddler's age, maturity, and emotional readiness. Generally, your toddler is ready for preschool if she can tolerate being away from you for short periods of time. If she seems bored or somewhat lonely at home because there are no other children with whom she can interact, you might consider preschool. On the other hand, a shy child can benefit from preschool by learning to overcome her discomfort in social situations.

Perhaps the best way to determine if your child is ready for preschool is to talk with other parents to learn about different preschools and to observe your child in social situations. You'll get a feel for whether she is ready and able to handle this new environment. If she isn't, don't despair. Usually a toddler who is not ready in the fall may be fully ready to attend a more occasional program, such as Mother's Day Out, by the beginning of the year. Your child is not "behind" simply because she isn't ready to go to preschool yet.

What to Look For In a Preschool

Once it is determined that your toddler is ready for preschool, the first step is to locate several programs that fit both your needs and your toddler's needs. Ask your pediatrician, your friends, and other trusted individuals about available programs. Ask them what they like and don't like about these programs. Don't take their opinions to the bank, however, because everyone has biases. If you know a parent who is on the same wavelength with you when it comes to parenting, discipline, and values,

> **Resist the urge to be taken in by a preschool program that is more glitter than substance. Often the best preschool is not necessarily the one with the best playground equipment or the most financial resources.**

you may want to consider her recommendation more seriously. Focus on what's important, don't let yourself be swept away by superficial things when making your decision.

Find out about the program itself. What is the school's philosophy about programs for toddlers? Is it a structured environment or more of a relaxed atmosphere? Does the school encourage independent learning, or must a toddler always work along with the group? Does the school offer a good bit of physical activity so that your toddler can let off steam? Will the school be sensitive to whatever special needs your toddler has?

What kinds of activities will your toddler be involved in? What can you expect her to learn? Is this a school that mainly encourages play, exploration, and basic skills acquisition, or does it have other expectations? Basic skills acquisition means introducing the toddler to her ABCs and simple counting. She may learn how to fold clothes or complete other chores and learn basic skills that will help her grow into greater independence and responsibility. As a general rule, if a preschool brags about its academic program, you may want to look elsewhere. Your toddler does not need academics as the mainstay of her preschool experience. She will have plenty of that in kindergarten!

Interviewing Preschools

Once you have narrowed your search to several preschools, it is time to make a visit. This is time consuming, but it will be to your advantage if you do so. Do not take your toddler with you, as this is not the time to be distracted by his reactions and antics. There will be time for that later. Instead call the preschool that you wish to visit and arrange for a tour. Most preschools are used to this type of request and rarely turn it down.

Important Considerations

At the preschool, find out whether or not the facility is licensed or registered and meets your state's requirements. The preschool that has fulfilled state requirements typically has a higher standard of care because they are required to provide it. This is not necessarily a reason to choose or dismiss a preschool as being appropriate for your child, but most parents feel more comfortable knowing that their preschool is being monitored.

Find out the hours of operation and determine whether the hours that are offered are a good fit for your child's body clock. Of course, cost has to be factored into your decision about which preschool your child will attend. Find out if the fees must be paid in full prior to your child's attendance or whether there is a payment plan. Some preschools offer a discount if you have more than one child attending the school.

Ask what the teacher-to-student ratio is for your toddler's prospective class. Some preschools are very large and have several teachers working in a single class. Generally, the younger the children, the lower the ratio should be. For example, for two- to almost-three-year-olds, experts consider the best ratio to be one adult to every four or five children. (Others recommend one adult for every five to seven three-year-olds.) Don't get so caught up in the ratio that you don't pay attention to whether all of the children are actually being monitored. A school can have many more teachers than are necessary for the number of children and still lack adequate supervision. Make sure that you're comfortable with the teacher-to-student interaction. Likewise, in a smaller preschool, you may find that the teacher-to-student ratio is a little higher. For example, some preschool programs have 10 to 12 students per class. Often there will be a teacher and a teacher's aide to accommodate the needs of these toddlers. This may be perfectly acceptable, depending on the amount of interaction the teacher and the aide actually have with the children.

Ask whether the teacher plans to have any contact with the parents. Will this be in the form of a conference or a telephone call? Is the parent allowed to call the teacher with concerns? Can you and the teacher communicate by e-mail? Practically every preschool has a policy regarding communicating with the parents, and you should find out what it is so that you can make use of the system from day one.

Are there any breaks so toddlers can rest or have a snack? How might toileting accidents be handled? How are children disciplined? Make a list of all the questions that you would like to have answered and take them with you. Most preschool directors who are comfortable with their policies and program will not hesitate to address any of your concerns.

As silly as it seems, some preschools have very strict entrance policies. Some actually test toddlers, although the concept seems somewhat laughable. If you're a parent who's very concerned about getting your child into this sort of day care, find out what the procedure is for evaluating your child. It will be up to you to decide whether or not your toddler is ready to be put into such a situation.

How does the school "feel"? In other words, do the kids there seem happy for the most part? Do the teachers appear to really enjoy what they are doing? Do you hear giggles, noises, and other sounds that let you know everyone is having a good time? Is it eerily quiet? Do the teachers seem overworked, tired, or grumpy? If the school "feels" right, you'll know it and this will be a good sign.

Getting Ready to Go!

You have finally chosen a preschool and made arrangements for your toddler to attend, and the first day is fast approaching. What should you do to prepare your toddler for this next step?

Much of what you've been doing with your toddler up to this point has in fact been preparing her for attending preschool. You have encouraged her to follow rules, taught her about sharing, and have involved her in activities with other children. In other words, your toddler is going to be about as ready as any other child. If your toddler has not been around a lot of other children, you might consider increasing her socializing time so that being around so many other children at preschool is not frightening.

Talking to Your Child About Preschool

If you are certain that your toddler is going to be attending preschool, start having casual conversations with her about it. Tell her that you have found a wonderful place for her to go so that she can play and learn with other children. Now you might contact the chosen preschool to request permission to visit with your toddler.

Don't worry if your toddler is somewhat intimidated by the atmosphere. Not only is it a new experience for her, but it is likely to be quite overwhelming. Your main goals are to show her where she will be going, introduce her to her teacher if possible, and help her to become familiar with the environment.

Once you've done this, try to incorporate more comments about preschool into your conversations. Be positive and enthusiastic when discussing it. Never, ever tell your toddler that you are going to miss her while she is gone. Although it may be true, your toddler does not need to sense any fear or apprehension from you. She needs to look at preschool as an opportunity for fun and to look forward to attending there.

First Day of School

If you're lucky, you'll have one of those toddlers who walk right into the schoolroom and never look back. Although it may hurt your feelings a bit that she doesn't seem to mind leaving you, it is also wonderful that she has such a sense of security and independence that new experiences like this do not frighten her. If you have a toddler who may have some difficulty separating from you, there are several things you can do to ease the transition.

First, find out if parents are allowed to stay for the first few days of preschool. If it is allowed and your toddler needs it, spend a few minutes with her before you leave. Before leaving, reassure her that you are coming back. Although your presence during the first few days should be quite active, you should work on becoming part of the background as quickly as possible. You do not want your toddler to think that going to preschool is for you *and* her. Let her begin to approach the schoolroom and activities without you. You might stand at the back of the room while she plays, giving her the security that you are close by but allowing her some independence as well. Consider taking a book, magazine, or something else you can do so that you won't appear to be staring at your toddler or make the teacher nervous.

Eventually it will be time to say goodbye to your toddler and actually leave. Acknowledge to your toddler that sometimes goodbyes are hard. Trying to argue that point with her is useless! Try to remain as upbeat as possible and point out the people she now knows by name. Show her all the fun things she will be doing there. Start guiding her to the teacher with whom you'll be leaving her so that she feels there is a grown-up she can count on. Then, when it's time for you to go, make your final goodbye short and sweet. Cheerfully tell your toddler to have fun, that you will be back soon, and that you love her. Leaving is very hard for a parent to do and often causes more distress for the parent than the toddler.

> **Whatever you do, try not to react to her tears by becoming upset or frustrated. When you do so, a toddler immediately assumes that there's something to be afraid of or something to dread. This will not make the separation between the two of you any easier.**

Handling Separation Anxiety

If you're unsure about how your toddler will handle your leaving, ask the teacher if there is a way for you to observe without your toddler knowing it. In this way, you can see if your toddler calms down quickly and begins to join in with the group or whether she cries helplessly. Ask the teacher if your toddler adjusts quickly to your departure or if her distress lasts throughout the morning and is just too much for her.

Make sure that everyone who takes your child to preschool (spouse, nanny, extended family) knows if there are any problems related to the separation. The last thing you need is for the other parent or another caregiver to be caught off-guard when it's time for them to leave. Make sure the teacher knows of any changes going on in your household that might make separation a little more difficult than usual. Don't assume that you are bothering the teacher by offering this information. Having an open line of communication between you and the teacher is the best way to ensure that your toddler will have a good preschool experience.

If your toddler does not seem to be getting used to her separation from you, there are several things to consider. Is she really comfortable in this setting? The situation may look fine to you, but that doesn't mean that your toddler feels good there. Is your toddler experiencing behavioral, sleep, or appetite changes? Some toddlers' behaviors change when they observe how other toddlers behave. This is not unusual, and you should probably expect your toddler to adopt some behaviors that you'd rather she didn't. However, if your toddler is increasingly clingy, is not sleeping, and is experiencing appetite changes, she may be under pressure. Preschool is not a time for a child to feel pressured and stressed.

Your Toddler and Her Teacher

Another thing to consider is the relationship between the toddler and her teacher. If your toddler does not seem at ease with the teacher after an appropriate amount of time has passed, there may be a problem. The length of time necessary to make this determination will depend on how well your particular child handles new situations, people, and places. The "fit" between teacher and child is important, and there are many reasons why it may not work. For example, your child's personality may clash with the teacher's personality,

> **The main thing to remember about preschool is that it should be fun. Your toddler is going through a wonderful stage of learning new things and exploring possibilities, and she has a natural curiosity about everything. The preschool experience should encourage this, not squelch it!**

and there's nothing wrong with this. Your child's teacher may not be especially nurturing and affectionate, characteristics your toddler is used to from your parenting. Any number of factors can influence the relationship between your toddler and her teacher. The bottom line is that the relationship should be a stable and warm one.

Final Considerations

If any of these concerns continue and are not alleviated by intervention or the passing of time, you should consider two things. First, is this the right preschool for your toddler? Often you're not going to know the answer to that question until your toddler has been there for some time. Do not try to talk yourself into "sticking it out," believing that it will get better. Trust your gut. If you feel this is a bad experience, find another preschool.

The second consideration is whether your toddler is actually ready for preschool. Depending on the number of problems she is experiencing at preschool, you may decide that she simply is not ready to leave home. If this appears to be the case, do not berate or blame yourself. Again, as with all things toddler, there is a lot of trial and error involved, and it may take some time before you find the right answer.

18

Having Fun!

Making Memories

Your toddler is only going to be a toddler for a short time. As you read this, you may be thinking, "Thank goodness!" But as parents with older kids have probably already told you, these are times that you just cannot get back. Many a family memory is made during toddlerhood, and much bonding occurs. Even though your job as a parent is a tough one, it's also very important for you and your toddler to have fun. While your toddler is playing, she is engaging in the most effective way to explore and learn. Different kinds of play promote the development of different skills, so choosing a broad range of activities is recommended.

Age-Appropriate Games and Toys

Your toddler is not going to like every single toy and game made available to her. Also, the box may say "For ages 2 through 4," but that doesn't mean your toddler will *only* play with that toy between those ages. What is fun for her now may not be fun next week. You'll have to work hard to keep up with your toddler's changing interests!

What's Best for your child?

Consider your child's skills and interests. For example, if she is interested in playing in the mud, she might enjoy play dough or another clay project. If she hates bugs, she is not going to want to take a nature walk. If she shows a particular talent for something and has fun doing it, follow her lead.

Age-Appropriateness

Most toys include a label that describe the minimum age at which a child should use the toy. Follow these labels closely; they are an important tool for keeping your toddler safe. Children may not be developmentally ready for a toy until they reach the appropriate age, so they shouldn't have access to it. If a child meets the minimum age requirement, but still does not enjoy the toy, put it away for a few months and try it again.

Tips for Picking Toys

When picking toys and activities, there are a few things to keep in mind. First, be aware of any small pieces that could be swallowed. Second, don't choose toys with sharp edges or points that can cut, poke, or scratch. Third, toys and activities should be designed for a toddler's short attention span. In other words, toys or games that require more concentration than your toddler is capable of are going to be useless. Fourth, as much as possible, encourage toys and activities that are interactive. Anything that engages her body and her mind will teach her new skills. Fifth, although most toys and activities should be interactive, pick a few that require her to be quiet. When a toddler looks through a book or colors at the kitchen table, she not only learns to pay attention, she also learns to play alone, which is a very important skill to develop.

Activities for Parents and Toddlers to Do Together

Obviously you can't have everything on hand for every activity, but there are a few things that no parent of a toddler should be without. If you have these five categories of supplies, you can entertain just about any toddler!

- Crayons, markers, and pencils
- Paper and coloring books
- White glue
- Washable paints
- Common household items that could have an imaginative use (cups, egg cartons, boxes, sacks, old socks, anything!)

The activities described below represent many of the familiar activities that we know and love plus new and different ones. You can pick one, adapt it to your own toddler, and take off. The activities are simple and are suitable for children ages 18 months and up. You'll notice that very few bells and whistles are necessary when it comes to entertaining your toddler. The point is for the two of you to have fun!

This Is the Way...

Sing the familiar song and add whatever activity it is you want your toddler to do. Sing, "This is the way we button our shirt, button our shirt..." or "This is the way we brush our teeth..." and so on. Actually, you can make up silly songs for all sorts of things. Toddlers love to giggle, and these kinds of activities are a great way to get them to cooperate!

Simon Says

No explanation needed—toddlers *do* love this time-tested favorite!

Look at Me!

Have your toddler lie down on a piece of large paper and draw a line around his body. When he gets up, give him crayons and tell him to color "himself." He can put on clothes, shoes, hair, and other items, and he can name all the body parts for you.

Making a Turkey

Trace around your toddler's outstretched hand on a piece of paper. Then show him how to make a turkey, a puppy, and other animals using this form. If you're feeling especially confident, help him glue on wings, a beak, or a puppy-dog tail made from other craft materials.

Do the Hokey Pokey

Again, no explanation needed, but this is another toddler favorite!

Puppets

Take an old sock or glove and gather some fun pieces of yarn, felt, and other materials to create a puppet. Use markers to draw the eyes and mouth, then glue (only the parent should handle the glue) on the decorations. Once it is complete, the two of you can put on a puppet show or simply have your puppets talks to each other.

Matching Shapes

Cut circle, square (or rectangle), and triangle shapes out of a piece of paper. Show them to your toddler and ask her to find things around the house that look like a circle, box, and triangle.

Make a Party Hat

Take two pieces of paper and place them end to end, overlapping them just enough to staple together (so you will have one long piece of paper). Roll the paper into a triangular cone, making sure the bottom fits your toddler's head. Cut off what you don't need and unroll the paper. Let your toddler decorate the paper and then re-form the hat shape and staple it together so she can wear it.

A Picture Frame

You can either make a frame out of cardboard or buy an undecorated one. Let your toddler decorate it as she wishes to hold a special picture. She might even want to give one away to a relative or friend as a gift.

Making Sandwiches

Gather the makings for your toddler's favorite sandwich. You can either let her help you make the sandwich or just make it yourself. Once done, give her a cookie cutter and help her to cut out that shape. Use geometrically shaped cookie cutters to teach her about shapes or animal cutters to teach her about animals. Sometimes, this activity can even encourage a picky eater to eat!

Make a Card

What grandmother or other cherished relative wouldn't love a card made just for them by your toddler? Get out the paper, markers, felt, yarn, and other scraps. Fold the paper into a card and let your toddler decorate it in any way she wishes. Ask her what she'd like you to write on it for her. Put it in an envelope, then place the stamp on it, and take her to the mailbox with you to mail it.

Nature Walk

Get a basket or a sack and take a walk with your toddler. Let her pick up interesting objects and place them in her container. Once she is home, take each object out and talk about it. She may then want to use some of them for an art project or just throw them out! A variation of this activity is to pick one type of object—for example, leaves, rocks, or feathers—and look only for those.

Things You Can Do with Boxes

There are so many things you can do with boxes, depending on their sizes.

- Decorate a box to hold a special item
- Make a hat
- Make a miniature or toddler-sized town and decorate the buildings using art supplies
- Make a car
- Make a house
- Make a kitchen complete with stove, refrigerator, and oven
- Make a head out of a box, drawing features on it with a marker or crayons

Dancing

Dancing is something just about every toddler likes to do. Your toddler can dance alone, with a partner, with props, or even with a costume. He can pretend he has an instrument, or the two of you can make up silly dances. All you need is music and a sense of fun!

Let's Pretend

The possibilities here are endless. With just an imagination, your toddler can pretend to be anything or anyone she wishes to be. Make up names, voices, jobs, clothes—anything! She can be as kooky or as realistic as she wants.

Make a Tent House

Cover the kitchen or dining-room table with a large sheet. If possible, cut holes in it to resemble windows in a house. Let your toddler crawl under the table and play in her "house." You might even join her!

Gardening

You might not want her to plan and arrange your plot, but she can still join in as you plant and tend to your garden. Give her two pots and let her fill them with dirt. Show her how to plant seeds or a small plant. Let her water her plants and watch them grow. Or let her help pick the flowers or vegetables from the garden while she names what she is picking.

Hide and Seek

There's the ordinary game of hide and seek—and then there's another way to play! Have your toddler gather three or four objects. Let her decide whether she wants to hide the objects and then let you find them, or if she'd rather you hide them and let her find them. Take turns and try to mix up the objects and hiding places as much as possible. Be sure to make the hiding spots places your toddler is likely to look so the game won't end in frustration and tears.

Macaroni Necklace

Take some yarn or string and let your toddler string macaroni on it to make a necklace. Make one for yourself and the two of you can wear them together.

Playing in the Sand

Take your toddler to the sandbox or to the beach. If you don't have a sandbox or a beach nearby, fill a large mixing bowl or box with sand and take it outdoors. Give your toddler cups, spoons, and muffin tins to use to make shapes, pretend food, and other fun things.

Resources

There are so many books, Web sites, TV programs, and information sources out there that it's hard to know how to pick the best ones when it comes to answering your questions and concerns about toddlers. The best rule is to go by your local bookstore or library and simply peruse the parenting section. You can do the same with the Internet. Look through several books and sites that look interesting to you. You do not have to buy or read everything you see. Instead, you may buy two or three books. When you read through them, most parents find that they pick a little something from each source.

Remember that parenting is an ongoing learning process. There is no one right way to parent. What *is* important is that you find information that will be useful and beneficial as you parent your own unique toddler. The following is a list of a few Web sites and books for you to refer to for additional information.

Agencies

National Academy of Early Childhood Programs—
    1834 Connecticut Avenue, NW, Washington, DC 20009.

National Association for the Education of Young Children —1313 L Street NW, Suite 500, Washington, DC 20005, (202) 232-8777, tollfree: (800) 424-2460 or (866) NAEYC-4U.

Books

Adesman, Andrew, Christine Adamec, and Susan Caughman. *Parenting Your Adopted Child: A Positive Approach to Building a Strong Family*. This book discusses some of the unique challenges of being the parent of an adopted child.

Barnes, Bridget A., Steven M. York, Ann Russell, and Father Flanagan's Boys Home. *Common Sense Parenting of Toddlers and Preschoolers*.

Brazelton, T. Berry. *Touchpoints*.

Cooke, Kaz. *Kid Wrangling: Real Guide to Caring for Babies, Toddlers, and Preschoolers*.

Douglas, Ann. *The Mother of All Toddler Books*.

Fields, Denise, and Ari Brown. *Toddler 411: Clear Answers and Smart Advice for Your Toddler*.

Karp, Harvey, and Paula Spencer. *The Happiest Toddler on the Block: The New Way to Stop the Daily Battle of Wills and Raise a Secure and Well-Behaved One-to-Four-Year-Old*.

Lyons, Elizabeth. *Ready or Not...There We Go!: The REAL Experts' Guide to the Toddler Years with Twins*.

Murphy, Jana. *The Secret Lives of Toddlers: A Parent's Guide to the Wonderful, Terrible, Fascinating Behavior of Children Ages 1–3*.

Peterson, Marion, and Diane Warner. *Single Parenting for Dummies*.

Phelan, Thomas W. *1-2-3 Magic: Effective Discipline for Children 2–12*.

Steinberg, Laurence. *The Ten Basic Principles of Good Parenting*.

Wilkoff, William. *How to Say No to Your Toddler: Creating a Safe, Rational, and Effective Discipline Program for Your 9-Month to 3-Year Old.*

Toddler Activity Books

Kohl, MaryAnn. *First Art: Art Experiences for Toddlers and Twos.*

McClure, Robin. *The Playskool Toddler's Busy Book.*

Rowley, Barbara. *Baby Days: Activities, Ideas, and Games for Enjoying Daily Life with a Child under Three.*

Schiller, Pam. *The Complete Resource Book for Toddlers and Twos: Over 2,000 Experiences and Ideas.*

Squibb, Betsy, Sally J. Dietz, and Jean Iker. *Learning Activities for Infants and Toddlers: An Easy Guide for Everyday Use (Creating Child-Centered Classrooms).*

Web sites

www.handinhandparenting.org

www.Kaboose.com

www.minti.com

www.MVParents.com

www.ParentingCatalog.com

www.RealLove.com

If you who are fortunate enough to have a toddler in your home, relax, get ready, and enjoy the ride of your life! On plenty of days, you won't believe you'll remain sane; but those days will pass, and the joy of having a toddler will return!

Index

B

C

E

F

M

N

O

P

R

S

T

U

V

Vacations, 173–181

Vagina, 55–57. *See also* Sexual issues

Verbalizing emotions, 71, 141, 155

Vision, 133–134

Vitamins, 51

Vocabulary, 63. *See also* Words

W

Waking up, 49

Walking, 3–5, 6–7, 45–47, 132, 213

Wandering eye, 134

Wandering from bed, 10

Washing hands, 59

Web sites, 175, 178, 180, 181, 219

Weight gain, little, 146

Wetting pants. *See* Accidents, toileting

Whining, 39, 113–114. *See also* Crying

Why questions, 63–64

Words, 15, 22–24, 23, 63

Working parents, 185, 189

Worry, 93, 186

Writing, 60

"Wrong," 126

About the Author

Rebecca Rutledge, Ph.D. is a clinical psychologist in Memphis, Tennessee. She has a private practice where she works with families and children. With children, she provides therapy and crisis management. She performs developmental, diagnostic and custodial evaluations. Additionally, she provides parenting seminars and helps divorcing parents with coparenting plans. She has written for several newspapers and is the author of *The Everything Parents Guide to Childhood Depression*, to be published by Adams Media in 2007.

Notes